2nd Grade

IOWA
MATH TEST PREP

Common Core State Standards

teachers' treasures, inc.

Copyright © 2014 Teachers' Treasures Inc.

Printed in the United States of America. All rights reserved. No part of this publication may be reproduced, stored in a retrieval system, or transmitted in any way or by any means (electronic, mechanical, photocopying, recording, or otherwise) without prior written permission from Teachers' Treasures, Inc., with the following exceptions:

Photocopying of student worksheets by a teacher who purchased this publication for his/her own class is permissible, but not for commercial resale. Reproduction of these materials for an entire school, or for a school system, is strictly prohibited. Reproduction of questions or book format by other state or commercial entities is strictly prohibited. Information taken directly from documents published by the Common Core State Standards Initiative is clearly indicated and not copyrighted.

Send all inquiries to:

sales@teacherstreasures.com
http://www.teacherstreasures.com

INTRODUCTION

Our 2nd Grade Math Test Prep for Common Core State Standards is an excellent resource to supplement your classroom's curriculum to assess and manage students' understanding of concepts outlined in the Common Core State Standards Initiative. This resource is divided into three sections: Diagnostic, Practice, and Assessment with multiple choice questions in each section. We recommend you use the Diagnostic section as a tool to determine the students' areas that need to be retaught. We also recommend you encourage your students to show their work to determine *how* and *why* the student arrived at an answer. The Practice section should be used to strengthen the students' knowledge by re-testing the standard to ensure comprehension of each standard. To ensure students' apply taught concepts in the classroom, we advise you use the Assessment section as a final test to verify the students' have mastered the standard.

This resource contains over 600 practice problems aligned to the Common Core State Standards. To view the standards, refer to pages *i* through *iii*.

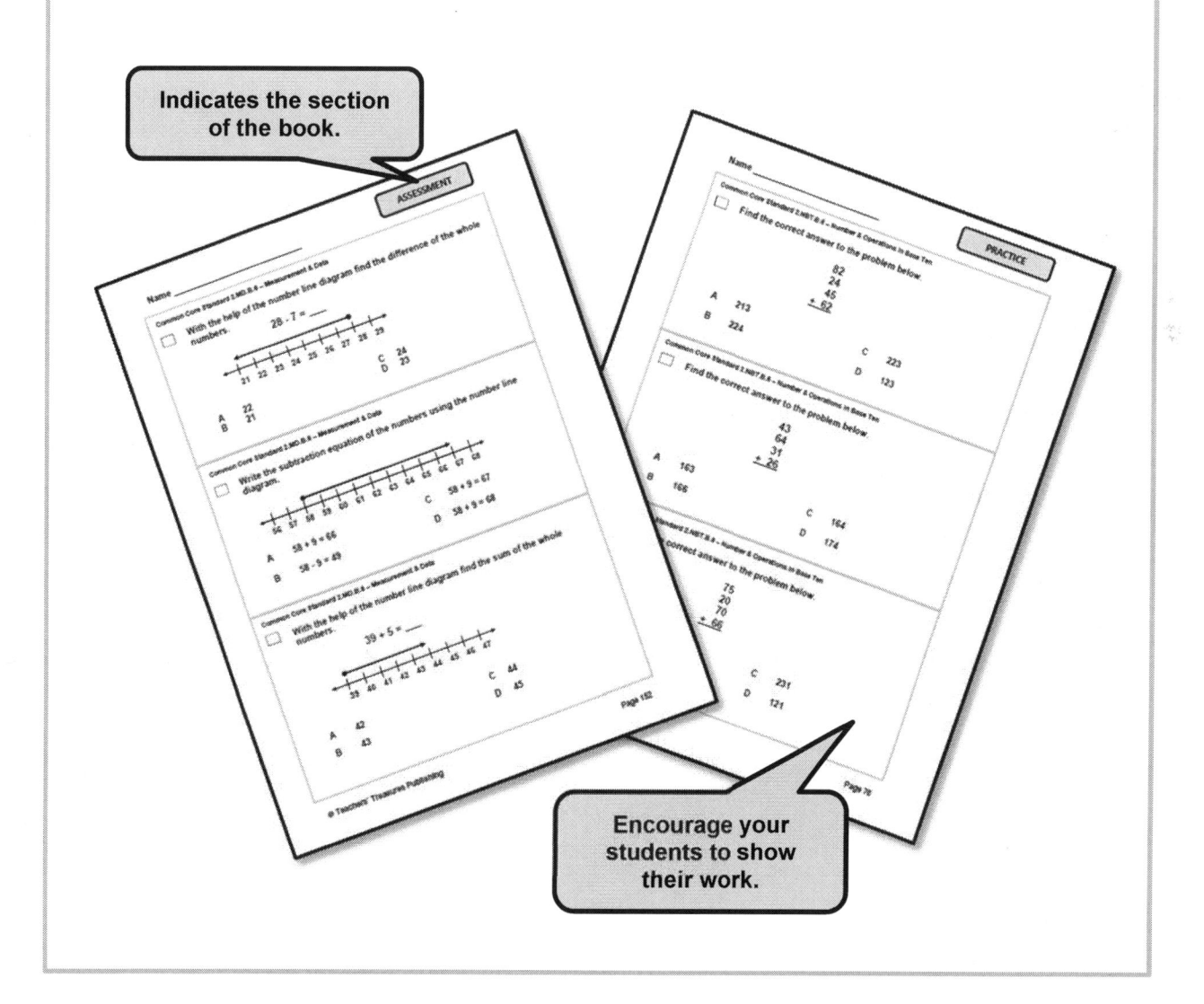

Indicates the section of the book.

Encourage your students to show their work.

© Teachers' Treasures Publishing

TABLE OF CONTENTS

2nd Grade
Math Test Prep
FOR
Common Core Standards

**Grade 2 Mathematics
Common Core State
Standards** ……... pages *i - iii*

**Operations & Algebraic Thinking
Practice Problems**
    2.OA.1 ………….. pages 1 – 8
    2.OA.2 ………….. pages 9 – 16
    2.OA.3 ………….. pages 17 – 24
    2.OA.4 ………….. pages 25 – 32

**Numbers & Operations in Base Ten
Practice Problems**
    2.NBT.1 ………….. pages 33 – 40
    2.NBT.2 ………….. pages 41 – 48
    2.NBT.3 ………….. pages 49 – 56
    2.NBT.4 ………….. pages 57 – 64
    2.NBT.5 ………….. pages 65 – 72
    2.NBT.6 ………….. pages 73 – 80
    2.NBT.7 ………….. pages 81 – 88
    2.NBT.8 ………….. pages 89 – 96
    2.NBT.9 ………….. pages 97 – 104

**Measurement & Data
Practice Problems**
    2.MD.1 ………….. pages 105 – 112
    2.MD.2 ………….. pages 113 – 120
    2.MD.3 ………….. pages 121 – 128
    2.MD.4 ………….. pages 129 – 136
    2.MD.5 ………….. pages 137 – 144
    2.MD.6 ………….. pages 145 – 152
    2.MD.7 ………….. pages 153 – 160
    2.MD.8 ………….. pages 161 – 168
    2.MD.9 ………….. pages 169 – 176
    2.MD.10 …………. pages 177 – 184

**Geometry
Practice Problems**
    2.G.1 ………….. pages 185 – 192
    2.G.2 ………….. pages 193 – 200
    2.G.3 ………….. pages 201 – 208

Answer Key ……………. pages 209 – 213

COMMON CORE STATE STANDARDS

Operations & Algebraic Thinking 2.OA

Represent and solve problems involving addition and subtraction.

1. Use addition and subtraction within 100 to solve one- and two-step word problems involving situations of adding to, taking from, putting together, taking apart, and comparing, with unknowns in all positions, e.g., by using drawings and equations with a symbol for the unknown number to represent the problem

Add and subtract within 20.

2. Fluently add and subtract within 20 using mental strategies.[2] By end of Grade 2, know from memory all sums of two one-digit numbers.

Work with equal groups of objects to gain foundations for multiplication.

3. Determine whether a group of objects (up to 20) has an odd or even number of members, e.g., by pairing objects or counting them by 2s; write an equation to express an even number as a sum of two equal addends.
4. Use addition to find the total number of objects arranged in rectangular arrays with up to 5 rows and up to 5 columns; write an equation to express the total as a sum of equal addends.

Number & Operations in Base Ten 2.NBT

Understand place value.

1. Understand that the three digits of a three-digit number represent amounts of hundreds, tens, and ones; e.g., 706 equals 7 hundreds, 0 tens, and 6 ones. Understand the following as special cases:

    A. 100 can be thought of as a bundle of ten tens — called a "hundred."
    B. The numbers 100, 200, 300, 400, 500, 600, 700, 800, 900 refer to one, two, three, four, five, six, seven, eight, or nine hundreds (and 0 tens and 0 ones).

2. Count within 1000; skip-count by 5s, 10s, and 100s.
3. Read and write numbers to 1000 using base-ten numerals, number names, and expanded form.
4. Compare two three-digit numbers based on meanings of the hundreds, tens, and ones digits, using >, =, and < symbols to record the results of comparisons.

Use place value understanding and properties of operations to add and subtract.

5. Fluently add and subtract within 100 using strategies based on place value, properties of operations, and/or the relationship between addition and subtraction.

COMMON CORE STATE STANDARDS

6. Add up to four two-digit numbers using strategies based on place value and properties of operations.
7. Add and subtract within 1000, using concrete models or drawings and strategies based on place value, properties of operations, and/or the relationship between addition and subtraction; relate the strategy to a written method. Understand that in adding or subtracting three-digit numbers, one adds or subtracts hundreds and hundreds, tens and tens, ones and ones; and sometimes it is necessary to compose or decompose tens or hundreds.
8. Mentally add 10 or 100 to a given number 100-900, and mentally subtract 10 or 100 from a given number 100-900.
9. Explain why addition and subtraction strategies work, using place value and the properties of operations.

Measurement & Data 2.MD

Measure and estimate lengths in standard units.

1. Measure the length of an object by selecting and using appropriate tools such as rulers, yardsticks, meter sticks, and measuring tapes.
2. Measure the length of an object twice, using length units of different lengths for the two measurements; describe how the two measurements relate to the size of the unit chosen.
3. Estimate lengths using units of inches, feet, centimeters, and meters.
4. Measure to determine how much longer one object is than another, expressing the length difference in terms of a standard length unit.

Relate addition and subtraction to length.

5. Use addition and subtraction within 100 to solve word problems involving lengths that are given in the same units, e.g., by using drawings (such as drawings of rulers) and equations with a symbol for the unknown number to represent the problem.
6. Represent whole numbers as lengths from 0 on a number line diagram with equally spaced points corresponding to the numbers 0, 1, 2, ..., and represent whole-number sums and differences within 100 on a number line diagram.

Work with time and money.

7. Tell and write time from analog and digital clocks to the nearest five minutes, using a.m. and p.m.6. Measure areas by counting unit squares (square cm, square m, square in, square ft, and improvised units).
8. Solve word problems involving dollar bills, quarters, dimes, nickels, and pennies, using $ and ¢ symbols appropriately. Example: If you have 2 dimes and 3 pennies, how many cents do you have?

COMMON CORE STATE STANDARDS

Represent and interpret data.

9. Generate measurement data by measuring lengths of several objects to the nearest whole unit, or by making repeated measurements of the same object. Show the measurements by making a line plot, where the horizontal scale is marked off in whole-number units.
10. Draw a picture graph and a bar graph (with single-unit scale) to represent a data set with up to four categories. Solve simple put-together, take-apart, and compare problems[1] using information presented in a bar graph.

Geometry 2.G

Reason with shapes and their attributes.

1. Recognize and draw shapes having specified attributes, such as a given number of angles or a given number of equal faces.[1] Identify triangles, quadrilaterals, pentagons, hexagons, and cubes.
2. Partition a rectangle into rows and columns of same-size squares and count to find the total number of them.
3. Partition circles and rectangles into two, three, or four equal shares, describe the shares using the words halves, thirds, half of, a third of, etc., and describe the whole as two halves, three thirds, four fourths. Recognize that equal shares of identical wholes need not have the same shape.

Name _____

DIAGNOSTIC

Common Core Standard 2.OA.A.1 – Operations & Algebraic Thinking

☑ Sydney loves to read. Last month she read 12 books. She read 4 novels, 3 magazines, 2 mystery books, and some history books. How many history books did she read?

A   2

(B)   3

C   4

D   5

Common Core Standard 2.OA.A.1 – Operations & Algebraic Thinking

☑ Ivan has 5 hats. His brother took 2, but later returned 1. How many hats does he have now?

A   5 – 2 - 1 = 2

(B)   5 – 2 + 1 = 4

C   1 + 1 + 5 = 7

D   2 + 5 + 1 = 8

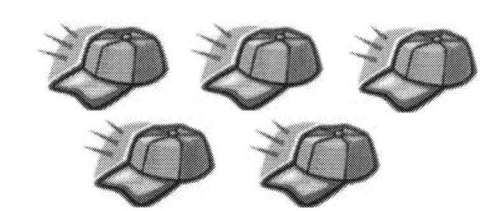

Common Core Standard 2.OA.A.1 – Operations & Algebraic Thinking

☑ Antonio took 33 shirts and 12 sweaters to a dry cleaner. How many pieces of clothing did he take to the dry cleaner?

A   12 + 30 = 42

B   12 + 32 = 44

(C)   33 + 12 = 45

D   45 - 12 = 33

© Teachers' Treasures Publishing

Name _____

DIAGNOSTIC

Common Core Standard 2.OA.A.1 – Operations & Algebraic Thinking

Andrew ordered 7 milkshakes. His sister drank 3 of the milkshakes. How many milkshakes does he have now?

- A   7 + 3 = 10
- B   4 + 3 = 7
- C   7 - 4 = 3
- (D)   7 - 3 = 4

Common Core Standard 2.OA.A.1 – Operations & Algebraic Thinking

Ryan had 12 balloons. He gave 6 balloons to his best friend Michael. How many balloons does he have now?

- A   5
- B   4
- (C)   6
- D   3

Common Core Standard 2.OA.A.1 – Operations & Algebraic Thinking

Devi has to inflate 100 balloons for a surprise birthday party at 1:00 PM. By 12:00 PM, she has blown up 33. How many more balloons does she have to inflate in the remaining time?

- A   100 + 33 = 133
- B   100 – 22 = 78
- C   22 + 33 = 55
- (D)   100 - 33 = 67

Name _____

PRACTICE

Common Core Standard 2.OA.A.1 – Operations & Algebraic Thinking

☐ The Zoo has 6 adult monkeys and 4 baby monkeys. How many monkeys are there in total at the Zoo?

A   6 - 4 = 2

(B)   6 + 4 = 10

C   10 - 2 = 8

D   10 - 5 = 5

Common Core Standard 2.OA.A.1 – Operations & Algebraic Thinking

☐ Francis picks 42 of the 98 strawberries in his garden. How many strawberries are there left for him to pick in the garden?

A   98 + 42 = 140

B   42 + 98 = 140

(C)   98 - 42 = 56

D   140 - 42 = 98

Common Core Standard 2.OA.A.1 – Operations & Algebraic Thinking

☐ On the first stop 9 children got off the school bus. On the second stop 7 more children got off the bus. 12 children remained on the bus waiting for their stop. How many children were on the bus in the beginning?

(A)   28

B   16

C   25

D   21

© Teachers' Treasures Publishing   Page 3

Name _____

PRACTICE

Common Core Standard 2.OA.A.1 – Operations & Algebraic Thinking

Greg wants to collect 80 baseball cards. He already has 48 cards. How many more baseball cards does he need to collect to reach 80?

A   80 + 48 = 128

B   128 - 80 = 48

C   128 - 48 = 80

D   80 - 48 = 32

Common Core Standard 2.OA.A.1 – Operations & Algebraic Thinking

Amanda planted 32 flowers in her garden. She planted 15 roses, 6 tulips, and some daisies. How many daisies did Amanda plant?

A   10

B   11

C   9

D   8

Common Core Standard 2.OA.A.1 – Operations & Algebraic Thinking

Farmer McDonald had 10 pigs on his farm. Two pigs ran away. How many pigs does the farmer have left?

A   5 + 5 = 10   C   10 - 8 = 2

B   10 - 5 = 5   D   10 - 2 = 8

© Teachers' Treasures Publishing   Page 4

Name _Mariana June 1_

PRACTICE

Common Core Standard 2.OA.A.1 – Operations & Algebraic Thinking

☐ **Jamal had 18 lollipops. He gave 3 lollipops to his little sister and 4 lollipops to his older brother. How many lollipops does he have left?**

A 7

B 10

Ⓒ 11

D 5

Common Core Standard 2.OA.A.1 – Operations & Algebraic Thinking

☐ **Bryson caught 17 fish on the first day, 12 fish on the second day, and 9 fish on the third day of his vacation. He put 7 fish back in the pond because they were too small and kept the rest in his net. How many fish did Bryson have in his net in all?**

A 30

B 32

Ⓒ 31

D 21

Common Core Standard 2.OA.A.1 – Operations & Algebraic Thinking

☐ **Rita practiced her dance routine 6 times at home and 8 times at her dance studio with her class. How many times did she practice her dance routine?**

Ⓐ 6 + 8 = 14

B 8 - 6 = 2

C 8 + 8 = 16

D 14 - 8 = 6

© Teachers' Treasures Publishing

Name _____

PRACTICE

Common Core Standard 2.OA.A.1 – Operations & Algebraic Thinking

☐ **Cameron wants to buy a video game that costs $43. He has saved $26 so far. How much more money does he need to save to buy the game?**

A   15

B   27

C   26

(D)   17

Common Core Standard 2.OA.A.1 – Operations & Algebraic Thinking

☐ **Abby had 5 toy frogs. Her mom bought her 3 more. How many toy frogs does Abby have now?**

A   8 + 3 = 11

(B)   5 + 3 = 8

C   8 + 5 = 13

D   11 - 3 = 8

Common Core Standard 2.OA.A.1 – Operations & Algebraic Thinking

☐ **Mirabai baked 48 cookies and her family ate 26 of them. How many cookies are left?**

A   48 + 26 = 74

(B)   48 - 26 = 22

C   26 + 74 = 100

D   22 + 48 = 70

© Teachers' Treasures Publishing

Name _____

ASSESSMENT

Common Core Standard 2.OA.A.1 – Operations & Algebraic Thinking

☐ The pet store had 14 bunnies for sale. Eight of the bunnies were sold over the weekend. How many bunnies will the store have for sale on Monday?

- (A) 14 - 8 = 6
- B 8 + 14 = 22
- C 8 + 22 = 30
- D 14 - 6 = 8

Common Core Standard 2.OA.A.1 – Operations & Algebraic Thinking

☐ Hasmik bought 6 flowers for her mother on Mother's Day. Her brother bought 8 flowers for their mother. How many flowers did their mother receive on Mother's Day?

- A 12
- B 13
- (C) 14
- D 15

Common Core Standard 2.OA.A.1 – Operations & Algebraic Thinking

☐ There are 21 balls in the gym. Eight are soccer balls and seven are basketballs. The rest are volleyballs. How many volleyballs are there?

- (A) 6
- B 4
- C 5
- D 7

Name _____

ASSESSMENT

Common Core Standard 2.OA.A.1 – Operations & Algebraic Thinking

☐ Mr. Meeks' class has 26 students, 15 of them are girls. How many boys are in Mr. Meeks' class?

A   26 - 15 = 11

B   26 - 11 = 15

C   11 + 15 = 25

D   15 - 11 = 4

Common Core Standard 2.OA.A.1 – Operations & Algebraic Thinking

☐ Alex has 35 red racecars and 24 yellow racecars. How many more red racecars does Alex have than yellow ones?

A   35 + 24 = 59

B   59 - 35 = 24

C   24 + 12 = 36

D   35 - 24 = 11

Common Core Standard 2.OA.A.1 – Operations & Algebraic Thinking

☐ The local sports store had 22 bicycles. On the first day they sold 5 bicycles. The next day they sold 7 more. How many bicycles are left at the store?

A   11

B   12

C   10

D   9

Name _Mariama June 2nd_

DIAGNOSTIC

Common Core Standard 2.OA.B.2 – Operations & Algebraic Thinking

☐ **Add following numbers below:**

$$\begin{array}{r} 15 \\ +\ 12 \\ \hline 27 \end{array}$$

- A   26
- (B) 27
- C   37
- D   36

Common Core Standard 2.OA.B.2 – Operations & Algebraic Thinking

☐ **Add the number at the top of the table to each of the numbers in the left column to find the correct answer below.**

12
+ 16

26

- A   25, 29
- B   27, 29
- (C) 27, 28
- D   24, 27

Add 16	
11	
12	

Common Core Standard 2.OA.B.2 – Operations & Algebraic Thinking

☐ **Subtract the following numbers below:**

17 - 4 = ____

- A   12
- B   17
- C   15
- (D) 13

Page 9

Name _____

DIAGNOSTIC

Common Core Standard 2.OA.B.2 – Operations & Algebraic Thinking

☐ **Subtract the following numbers below:**

$$\begin{array}{r} 19 \\ -\ 16 \\ \hline \end{array}$$

(A) 3   C 4

B 2   D 1

Common Core Standard 2.OA.B.2 – Operations & Algebraic Thinking

☐ **Subtract the number at the top of the table from each of the numbers in the left column to find the correct answer below.**

A 10, 11

B 9, 22

C 10, 23

(D) 10, 22

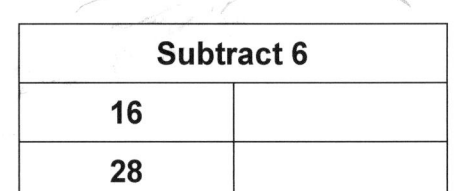

Subtract 6	
16	
28	

Common Core Standard 2.OA.B.2 – Operations & Algebraic Thinking

☐ **Fill in the missing numbers in the addition problem below.**

★★★★★ + ★★★ = ★★★★ + ★★★★
★★★★   ★   ★★   ★★★

7 + ___ = 5 + ___

A 2 and 5   (C) 3 and 5

B 4 and 3   D 3 and 4

Name _____

PRACTICE

Common Core Standard 2.OA.B.2 – Operations & Algebraic Thinking

☐ **Add the following numbers below:**

$$\begin{array}{r} 21 \\ +\ 17 \\ \hline \end{array}$$

A 38

B 48

C 37

D 36

Common Core Standard 2.OA.B.2 – Operations & Algebraic Thinking

☐ **Add the number at the top of the table to each of the numbers in the left column to find the correct answer below.**

35, 29

36, 27

27, 25

27, 45

Add 15	
21	
12	

Common Core Standard 2.OA.B.2 – Operations & Algebraic Thinking

☐ **Fill in the missing numbers in the addition problem below.**

◆◆◆◆ + ◆◆◆◆ = ◆◆◆ + ◆◆◆◆◆◆

6 + ___ = ___ + 9

A   4 and 3   C   6 and 3

B   6 and 6   D   4 and 6

© Teachers' Treasures Publishing

Name _____

PRACTICE

Common Core Standard 2.OA.B.2 – Operations & Algebraic Thinking

☐ Subtract the following numbers below:

$$\begin{array}{r} 25 \\ -\ 17 \\ \hline \end{array}$$

(A)   8   C   18

B   7   D   12

Common Core Standard 2.OA.B.2 – Operations & Algebraic Thinking

☐ Subtract the number at the top of the table from each of the numbers in the left column to find the correct answer below.

A   13, 21

B   15, 15

(C) 15, 22

D   10, 22

Subtract 11	
26	
33	

Common Core Standard 2.OA.B.2 – Operations & Algebraic Thinking

☐ Add the following numbers below:

45 + 6 = ____

A   55   C   49

B   41   (D)   51

© Teachers' Treasures Publishing   Page 12

Name _____

PRACTICE

Common Core Standard 2.OA.B.2 – Operations & Algebraic Thinking

☐ **Add the following numbers below:**

$$\begin{array}{r} 17 \\ +\ 5 \\ \hline \end{array}$$

  A   25

  B   23

  C   27

  (D) 22

Common Core Standard 2.OA.B.2 – Operations & Algebraic Thinking

☐ **Add the number at the top of the table to each of the numbers in the left column to find the correct answer below.**

  (A) 24, 52

  B   24, 53

  C   25, 52

  D   24, 62

Add 7	
17	
45	

Common Core Standard 2.OA.B.2 – Operations & Algebraic Thinking

☐ **Subtract the following numbers below:**

13 - 4 = ____

  A   8   C   11

  (B) 9   D   10

© Teachers' Treasures Publishing   Page 13

Name _____

PRACTICE

Common Core Standard 2.OA.B.2 – Operations & Algebraic Thinking

☐ Subtract the following numbers below:

$$\begin{array}{r} 30 \\ -\ 14 \\ \hline \end{array}$$

A   18

B   17

C   14

(D)   16

Common Core Standard 2.OA.B.2 – Operations & Algebraic Thinking

☐ Subtract the number at the top of the table from each of the numbers in the left column to find the correct answer below.

(A)   6, 18

B   6, 28

C   15, 18

D   6, 36

Subtract 9	
15	
27	

Common Core Standard 2.OA.B.2 – Operations & Algebraic Thinking

☐ Fill in the missing numbers in the addition problem below.

♥♥♥♥ + ♥♥♥ = ♥♥ + ♥♥♥♥♥

4 + ___ = 2 + ___

A   2 and 5   C   3 and 4

(B)   3 and 5   D   4 and 5

© Teachers' Treasures Publishing

Name _____

ASSESSMENT

Common Core Standard 2.OA.B.2 – Operations & Algebraic Thinking

☐ **Add the following numbers below:**

$$\begin{array}{r} 44 \\ +\ 9 \\ \hline \end{array}$$

A   43

B   44

C   53

D   54

Common Core Standard 2.OA.B.2 – Operations & Algebraic Thinking

☐ **Add the number at the top of the table to each of the numbers in the left column to find the correct answer.**

A   17, 22

B   16, 23

C   17, 23

D   18, 22

Add 8	
9	
15	

Common Core Standard 2.OA.B.2 – Operations & Algebraic Thinking

☐ **Subtract the following numbers below:**

50 – 24 = ____

A   26   C   34

B   36   D   16

© Teachers' Treasures Publishing

Name _____

ASSESSMENT

Common Core Standard 2.OA.B.2 – Operations & Algebraic Thinking

☐ **Subtract the following numbers below:**

$$\begin{array}{r} 14 \\ -6 \\ \hline \end{array}$$

A   18

B   9

(C)   8

D   20

Common Core Standard 2.OA.B.2 – Operations & Algebraic Thinking

☐ **Add the number at the top of the table to each of the numbers in the left column to find the correct answer below.**

A   24, 32

B   30, 25

C   25, 19

(D)   20, 25

Add 13	
17	
12	

Common Core Standard 2.OA.B.2 – Operations & Algebraic Thinking

☐ **Fill in the missing numbers in the addition problem below.**

$$11 + 7 = \underline{} + 15$$

A   4   C   5

B   3   (D)   6

Name _____

DIAGNOSTIC

Common Core Standard 2.OA.C.3 – Operations & Algebraic Thinking

☐ Which of the following numbers are odd?

6, 3, 8, 15, 4, 16

A 3, 15
B 3, 6, 15
C 4, 6, 16
D 15, 16

Common Core Standard 2.OA.C.3 – Operations & Algebraic Thinking

☐ Which odd number completes the list below?

___, 3, 5, 7

A 0
B 2
C 1
D 9

Common Core Standard 2.OA.C.3 – Operations & Algebraic Thinking

☐ Count the objects below. What is the total number? Is it odd or even?

A 7 even
B 7 odd
C 6 even
D 5 odd

© Teachers' Treasures Publishing

Name _____

DIAGNOSTIC

Common Core Standard 2.OA.C.3 – Operations & Algebraic Thinking

☐ **Find an odd number that is greater than 24, but less than 27.**

    A   23

    B   26

    (C)   25

    D   21

Common Core Standard 2.OA.C.3 – Operations & Algebraic Thinking

☐ **Count the blocks below. Complete the equation to show the sum of the two equal numbers. Is it even or odd?**

$6 + 6 =$ _____

    A   11 Odd   (C)   12 Even

    B   10 Even   D   12 Odd

Common Core Standard 2.OA.C.3 – Operations & Algebraic Thinking

☐ **Count the shoes below into pairs. How many shoes are there? Is that number even or odd?**

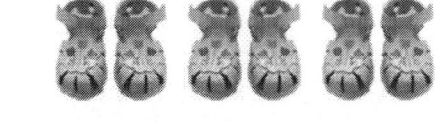

    (A)   12 even

    B   14 even

    C   12 odd

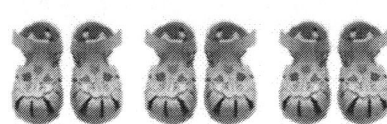

    D   14 odd

Name _____

PRACTICE

Common Core Standard 2.OA.C.3 – Operations & Algebraic Thinking

☐ Which of the following numbers are even?

0, 2, 5, 6, 9, 12, 15, 16

- A 2, 5, 6, 12, 16
- B 0, 2, 6, 9, 12
- (C) 0, 2, 6, 12, 16
- D 2, 6, 12, 16

Common Core Standard 2.OA.C.3 – Operations & Algebraic Thinking

☐ Find an odd number that is less than 11, but greater than 8.

- A 8
- (B) 10
- C 9
- D 11

Common Core Standard 2.OA.C.3 – Operations & Algebraic Thinking

☐ Counting by twos, count the number of phones below. Is it even or odd?

- (A) 11 odd
- B 11 even
- C 12 even
- D 12 odd

© Teachers' Treasures Publishing

Page 19

Name _____

PRACTICE

Common Core Standard 2.OA.C.3 – Operations & Algebraic Thinking

☐ Which of the following numbers are even?

21, 24, 27, 28, 33, 34, 38, 39

- A 21, 24, 28, 33
- (B) 24, 28, 34, 38
- C 24, 28, 34, 39
- D 24, 27, 28, 34

Common Core Standard 2.OA.C.3 – Operations & Algebraic Thinking

☐ Count the blocks below. Complete the equation to show the sum of the two equal numbers. Is it even or odd?

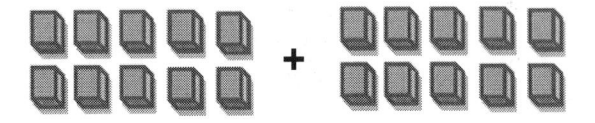

10 + 10 = ____

- (A) 20 Even
- B 10 Even
- C 20 Odd
- D 10 Odd

Common Core Standard 2.OA.C.3 – Operations & Algebraic Thinking

☐ Find an even number that comes before 32 and after 29.

- A 31
- (B) 30
- C 32
- D 28

© Teachers' Treasures Publishing

Page 20

Name _____

PRACTICE

Common Core Standard 2.OA.C.3 – Operations & Algebraic Thinking

☐ Identify the number of gloves counting by twos. Is it an odd or an even number?

A 14 even

B 10 odd

C 12 even

D 11 odd

Common Core Standard 2.OA.C.3 – Operations & Algebraic Thinking

☐ Find and shade all even numbers.

121	144	155	176
222	232	257	294
325	336	349	364

A 144, 176, 222, 232, 294, 336, 364

B 121, 144, 176, 222, 294, 325, 336

C 144, 176, 222, 232, 257, 336, 364

D 176, 222, 232, 294, 336, 349, 364

Common Core Standard 2.OA.C.3 – Operations & Algebraic Thinking

☐ Which even number comes next?

12, 14, 16, ____

A 14   C 20

B 12   D 18

© Teachers' Treasures Publishing

Page 21

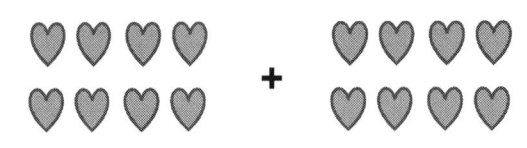

Name _____

PRACTICE

Common Core Standard 2.OA.C.3 – Operations & Algebraic Thinking

☐ **Complete the equation to show the sum of the two equal numbers.**

♥♥♥♥   ♥♥♥♥
♥♥♥♥   +   ♥♥♥♥

____ + ____ = 16

A   6 and 6   C   9 and 9

B   7 and 7   D   8 and 8

Common Core Standard 2.OA.C.3 – Operations & Algebraic Thinking

☐ **Find and shade all odd numbers.**

38	44	52	83
23	32	57	24
25	33	49	36

A   83, 23, 57, 25, 33, 49   C   23, 25, 33, 44, 49, 57

B   83, 44, 23, 32, 25, 49   D   38, 83, 23, 57, 25, 33

Common Core Standard 2.OA.C.3 – Operations & Algebraic Thinking

☐ **Count the objects below. Is the total number of airplanes even or odd?**

A   16 Even   C   14 Odd

B   18 Odd   D   14 Even

© Teachers' Treasures Publishing

Page 22

Name _____

ASSESSMENT

Common Core Standard 2.OA.C.3 – Operations & Algebraic Thinking

☐ Find an odd number that is greater than 13 and less than 16.

A   14

B   13

(C)   15

D   12

Common Core Standard 2.OA.C.3 – Operations & Algebraic Thinking

☐ Count the soccer balls below. Complete the equation to show the sum of the two equal numbers. Is that number even or odd?

____ + ____ = 22

A   10 Even   (C)   11 Odd

B   22 Even   D   9 Odd

Common Core Standard 2.OA.C.3 – Operations & Algebraic Thinking

☐ Find and shade all even numbers.

15	16	17	18
26	27	28	29

A   26, 27, 28, 29   C   15, 16, 17, 18

B   15, 17, 27, 29   (D)   16, 18, 26, 28

© Teachers' Treasures Publishing

Name _____

ASSESSMENT

Common Core Standard 2.OA.C.4 – Operations & Algebraic Thinking

☐ Which even number completes the list below?

_____, 56, 58, 60, 62

A   52

B   54

C   50

D   64

Common Core Standard 2.OA.C.4 – Operations & Algebraic Thinking

☐ Count how many chocolates there are in the box. Is that number even or odd?

A   18 Even   C   17 Odd

B   16 Even   D   19 Odd

Common Core Standard 2.OA.C.4 – Operations & Algebraic Thinking

☐ The sum of which two equal odd numbers will be equal to 26?

A   12

B   11

C   13

D   14

© Teachers' Treasures Publishing

Page 24

Name _____

DIAGNOSTIC

Common Core Standard 2.OA.C.4 – Operations & Algebraic Thinking

☐ **Write the addition sentence that matches the picture below.**

(A) ⃝   A   4 + 4 + 4 = 12   C   2 + 2 + 2 + 2 = 8

B   3 + 3 + 3 = 9   D   3 + 3 + 3 + 3 + 3 = 15

Common Core Standard 2.OA.C.4 – Operations & Algebraic Thinking

☐ **Write an addition sentence matching the smiley faces below.**

A   5 + 5 + 5 = 15   (C) ⃝   6 + 6 + 6 = 18

B   3 + 3 + 3 + 3 + 3 = 15   D   4 + 4 + 4 + 4 + 4 = 20

Common Core Standard 2.OA.C.4 – Operations & Algebraic Thinking

☐ **Write the addition sentence that matches the balloon picture below.**

(A) ⃝   A   6 + 6 = 12   C   6 + 6 + 6 = 18

B   2 + 2 + 2 + 2 + 2 = 10   D   4 + 4 + 4 + 4 = 16

© Teachers' Treasures Publishing   Page 25

Name _____

DIAGNOSTIC

Common Core Standard 2.OA.C.4 – Operations & Algebraic Thinking

☐ Which of the following describes the drawing below?

A	6 + 6 + 6 = 18
B	6 + 6 + 6 + 6 = 24
C	6 + 4 = 10
D	5 + 5 + 5 + 5 = 20

Common Core Standard 2.OA.C.4 – Operations & Algebraic Thinking

☐ Which addition sentence best represents the drawing below?

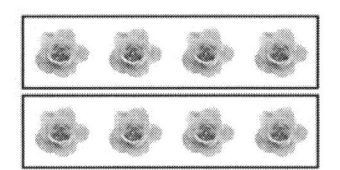

| A | 2 + 2 + 2 + 2 + 2 = 10 | C | 4 + 4 = 8 |
| B | 4 + 4 + 4 = 12 | D | 2 + 2 + 2 + 2 = 8 |

Common Core Standard 2.OA.C.4 – Operations & Algebraic Thinking

☐ Which equation best represents the drawing below?

| A | 5 + 2 = 7 | C | 10 + 2 = 12 |
| B | 5 + 5 + 5 = 15 | D | 5 + 5 = 10 |

© Teachers' Treasures Publishing

Page 26

Name _____

PRACTICE

Common Core Standard 2.OA.C.4 – Operations & Algebraic Thinking

☐ Which addition sentence best represents the picture below?

(A) 7 + 7 + 7 = 21   C   3 + 3 + 3 + 3 + 3 + 3 = 18

B   7 + 3 = 10   D   7 + 7 = 14

Common Core Standard 2.OA.C.4 – Operations & Algebraic Thinking

☐ Which of the following best describes the drawing below?

A   5 + 5 + 5 + 5 = 20   C   10 + 10 = 20

(B) 5 + 5 + 5 = 15   D   3 + 3 + 3 = 9

Common Core Standard 2.OA.C.4 – Operations & Algebraic Thinking

☐ Arin baked some cakes. She arranged them in two rows and four columns. How many cakes did she bake?

(A) 4 + 4 = 8   C   3 + 3 + 3 = 6

B   2 + 2 + 2 = 6   D   2 + 2 + 2 + 2 + 2 = 10

© Teachers' Treasures Publishing

Name ______________________________

PRACTICE

Common Core Standard 2.OA.C.4 – Operations & Algebraic Thinking

☐ **Matthew arranged some beach balls into 2 rows and 3 columns. How many beach balls does he have altogether?**

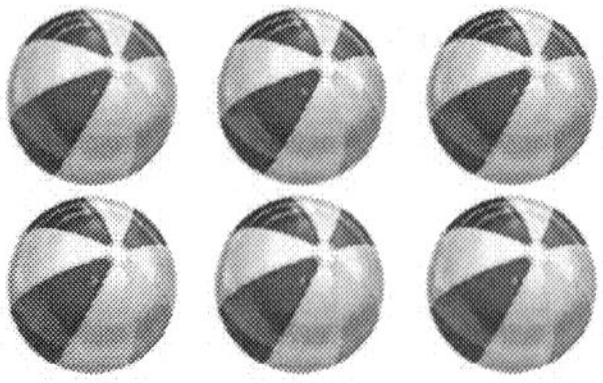

A 3 + 3 = 6

B 2 + 3 = 5

C 2 + 2 + 2 = 6

D 3 + 3 + 3 = 9

Common Core Standard 2.OA.C.4 – Operations & Algebraic Thinking

☐ **Which of the following drawings represents the addition problem?**

4 + 4 + 4 = 12

A 

B 

C 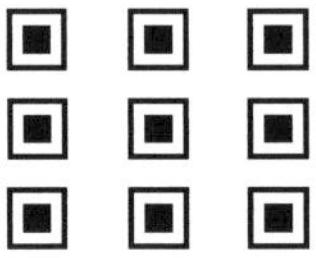

D 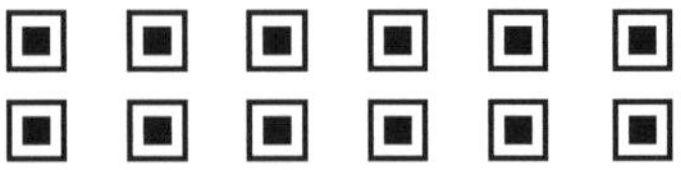

Common Core Standard 2.OA.C.4 – Operations & Algebraic Thinking

☐ **Which of the following best represents the drawing below?**

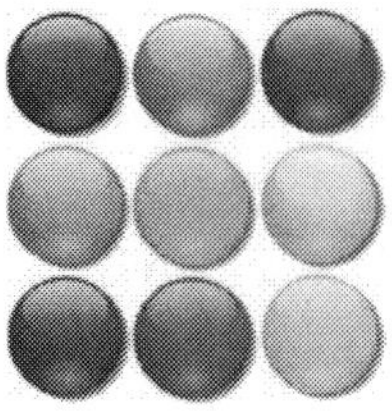

A 3 + 3 =6

B 3 + 3 + 3 = 9

C 3 + 3 + 3 + 3 = 12

D 3 + 4 = 7

Name _____

PRACTICE

Common Core Standard 2.OA.C.4 – Operations & Algebraic Thinking

☐ Which addition sentence best represents the picture below?

A   3 + 3 + 3 + 3 + 3 + 3 = 18

B   8 + 8 = 16

C   3 + 8 = 11

(D)   8 + 8 + 8 = 24

Common Core Standard 2.OA.C.4 – Operations & Algebraic Thinking

☐ Aubrey was arranging pastries in a box. She placed them in 3 rows and 5 columns. How many pastries did she put in the box?

(A)   5 + 5 + 5 = 15

B   3 + 5 = 8

C   4 + 4 + 4 + 4 = 16

D   3 + 3 + 3 + 3 + 12

Common Core Standard 2.OA.C.4 – Operations & Algebraic Thinking

☐ Which of the following represents the addition problem below?

6 + 6 = 12

A

(B)

C

D

© Teachers' Treasures Publishing   Page 29

Name __Mariana June 3, 2019__

PRACTICE

Common Core Standard 2.OA.C.4 – Operations & Algebraic Thinking

☐ Look at the drawing below. Which answer best describes the drawing?

(A) 5 + 5 + 5 + 5 + 5 = 25   C   5 + 4 = 9

B   5 + 5 + 5 + 5 = 20   D   4 + 4 + 4 + 4 + 4 = 20

Common Core Standard 2.OA.C.4 – Operations & Algebraic Thinking

☐ Heather arranged her candies in 4 rows and 4 columns. Which answer below best describes how Heather arranged the candies?

A   8 + 8 + 8 + 8 = 32   C   4 + 4 = 8

B   4 + 4 + 4 + 4 + 4 = 20   (D) 4 + 4 + 4 + 4 = 16

Common Core Standard 2.OA.C.4 – Operations & Algebraic Thinking

☐ Which picture best describes the following problem below?

5 + 5 + 5 = 15

A   (C)

B   D

© Teachers' Treasures Publishing

Page 30

Name _____

ASSESSMENT

Common Core Standard 2.OA.C.4 – Operations & Algebraic Thinking

☐ Which addition sentence best represents the picture below?

A   4 + 4 + 4 + 4 + 4 + 4 = 24

C   7 + 7 + 7 = 21

(B) 7 + 7 + 7 + 7 = 28

D   4 + 7 = 11

Common Core Standard 2.OA.C.4 – Operations & Algebraic Thinking

☐ Which of the following best represents 5 + 5 = 10?

A

C

(B)

D

Common Core Standard 2.OA.C.4 – Operations & Algebraic Thinking

☐ An egg carton has 2 rows of 6 eggs. How many eggs are in the carton altogether?

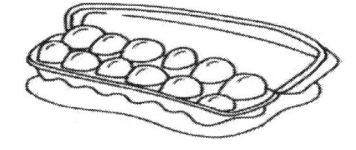

(A) 12

C   13

B   11

D   14

© Teachers' Treasures Publishing

Page 31

Name _____

ASSESSMENT

Common Core Standard 2.OA.C.4 – Operations & Algebraic Thinking

Helen's grandmother arranged her slippers into 2 rows of 3 pairs of slippers. Which answer below best describes how the slippers were arranged?

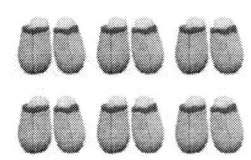

A   3 + 3 = 6   C   3 + 3 + 3 = 9

B   2 + 2 + 2 = 6   D   2 + 2 + 2 + 2 + 2 + 2 = 12

Common Core Standard 2.OA.C.4 – Operations & Algebraic Thinking

Which of the number sentences best represents the drawing below?

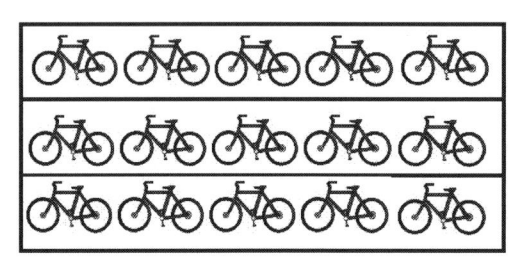

A   3 + 5 = 15   C   3 + 3 + 3 + 3 = 12

B   5 + 5 = 10   D   5 + 5 + 5 = 15

Common Core Standard 2.OA.C.4 – Operations & Algebraic Thinking

Which picture best describes the following problem?

3 + 3 + 3 = 9

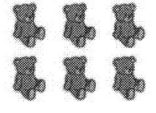

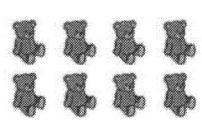

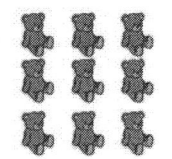

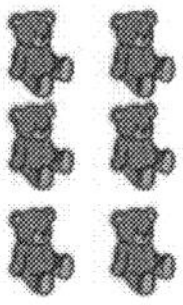

© Teachers' Treasures Publishing   Page 32

Name _____

DIAGNOSTIC

Common Core Standard 2.NBT.A.1 – Number & Operations in Base Ten

☐ Which answer best fits the model below?

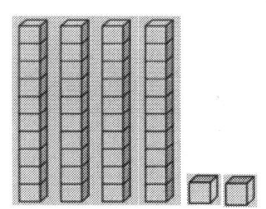

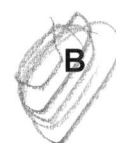

| A | 44 | C | 41 |
| B | 42 | D | 32 |

Common Core Standard 2.NBT.A.1 – Number & Operations in Base Ten

☐ What is the value of the underlined digit below?

213

| A | 3 tens | C | 3 hundreds |
| B | 3 ones | D | 2 ones |

Common Core Standard 2.NBT.A.1 – Number & Operations in Base Ten

☐ What number is shown by the place value model below?

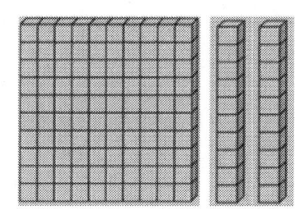

| A | 120 | C | 100 |
| B | 110 | D | 111 |

© Teachers' Treasures Publishing

Page 33

Name _____

DIAGNOSTIC

Common Core Standard 2.NBT.A.1 – Number & Operations in Base Ten

☐ What is the value of the underlined digit?

<u>8</u>45

- A   8 tens
- B   8 ones
- (C)   8 hundreds
- D   8 thousands

Common Core Standard 2.NBT.A.1 – Operations & Algebraic Thinking

☐ Which place value model shows 6 ones?

- A   ▢▢▢▢
- (C)   ▢▢▢▢▢▢
- B   ▢▢▢▢▢
- D   ▢▢▢▢▢▢▢

Common Core Standard 2.NBT.A.1 – Number & Operations in Base Ten

☐ Fill in the missing numbers below.

sixty two = ____ tens and ____ ones

- A   5 tens and 2 ones
- B   6 tens and 3 ones
- C   6 tens and 5 ones
- (D)   6 tens and 2 ones

© Teachers' Treasures Publishing

Name _____

PRACTICE

Common Core Standard 2.NBT.A.1 – Number & Operations in Base Ten

☐ What is the value of the model below?

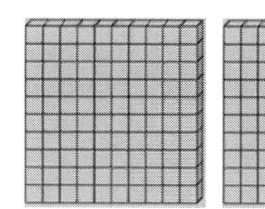

A   20

B   2,000

C   200

D   230

Common Core Standard 2.NBT.A.1 – Operations Number & Operations in Base Ten

☐ What is the value of the underlined digit below?

6<u>7</u>8

A   7 tens

B   7 ones

C   6 hundreds

D   7 hundreds

Common Core Standard 2.NBT.A.1 – Number & Operations in Base Ten

☐ Find the total value of the blocks below.

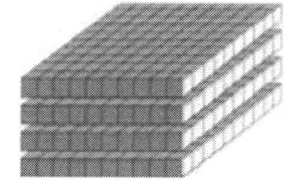

A   320

B   420

C   402

D   422

© Teachers' Treasures Publishing

Name _____

PRACTICE

Common Core Standard 2.NBT.A.1 – Number & Operations in Base Ten

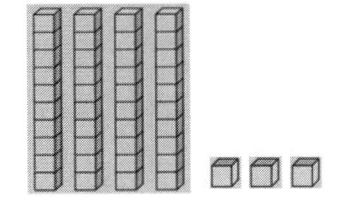

Find the correct answer to the problem below.

7 hundreds = _____ ones.

A   70
B   700
C   7
D   7,000

Common Core Standard 2.NBT.A.1 – Number & Operations in Base Ten

What is the value of the model below?

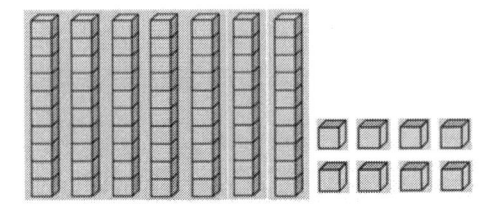

A   78
B   76
C   68
D   66

Common Core Standard 2.NBT.A.1 – Number & Operations in Base Ten

Which place value model below shows 53?

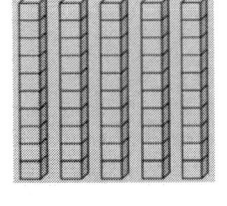

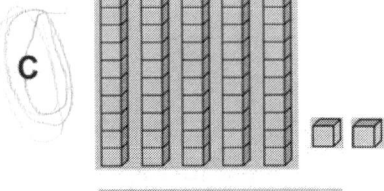

A
B
C
D

© Teachers' Treasures Publishing

Name _____

PRACTICE

Common Core Standard 2.NBT.A.1 – Number & Operations in Base Ten

☐   Find the correct answer to the problem below.

4 hundreds = _____ tens.

A   4

B   400

C   4,000

D   40

Common Core Standard 2.NBT.A.1 – Number & Operations in Base Ten

☐   What is the value of the underlined digit?

<u>2</u>341

A   2 tens

B   3 ones

C   3 hundreds

D   2 thousands

Common Core Standard 2.NBT.A.1 – Number & Operations in Base Ten

☐   Find the total value of the blocks below.

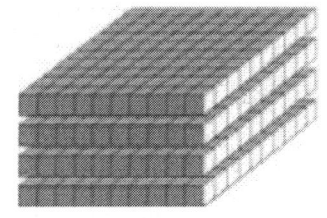

A   300   C   500

B   400   D   4,000

© Teachers' Treasures Publishing   Page 37

Name _____

PRACTICE

Common Core Standard 2.NBT.A.1 – Number & Operations in Base Ten

☐ Which place value model shows 102 below?

A

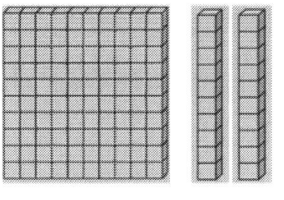

B

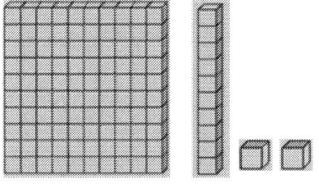

C

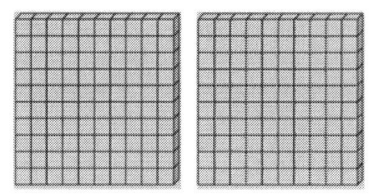

D

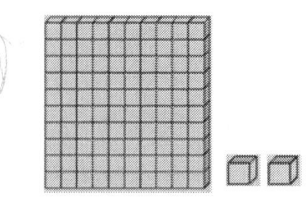

Common Core Standard 2.NBT.A.1 – Number & Operations in Base Ten

☐ Find the correct answer to the problem below.

5 hundreds = _____ ones.

A   5

B   50

C   500

D   5,000

Common Core Standard 2.NBT.A.1 – Number & Operations in Base Ten

☐ Find the total value of the blocks below.

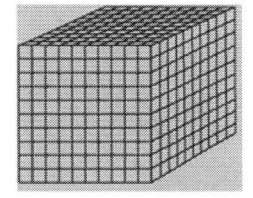

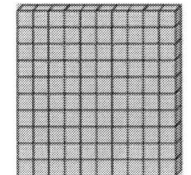

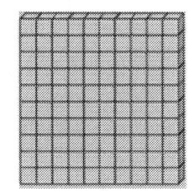

A   120   C   1,002

B   1020   D   1,200

© Teachers' Treasures Publishing

Name _____

ASSESSMENT

Common Core Standard 2.NBT.A.1 – Number & Operations in Base Ten

☐ What is the value of the underlined digit?

5<u>9</u>7

(A)   9 tens

B   7 ones

C   9 hundreds

D   9 ones

Common Core Standard 2.NBT.A.1 – Number & Operations in Base Ten

☐ Which place value model shows 44?

(A)

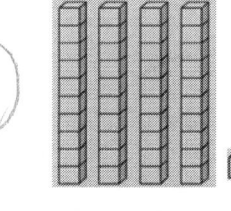

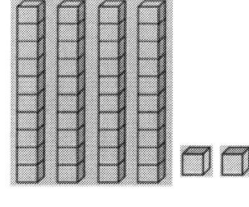

B

C

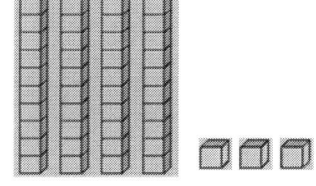

D

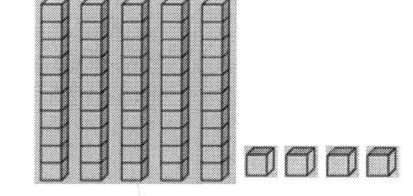

Common Core Standard 2.NBT.A.1 – Number & Operations in Base Ten

☐ Fill in the missing numbers below.

seventy eight = ____ tens and ____ ones

A   7 tens and 9 ones

(B)   7 tens and 8 ones

C   8 tens and 7 ones

D   8 tens and 8 ones

© Teachers' Treasures Publishing

Name __June 6, 2019__

ASSESSMENT

Common Core Standard 2.NBT.A.1 – Number & Operations in Base Ten

☐ Find the total value of the blocks.

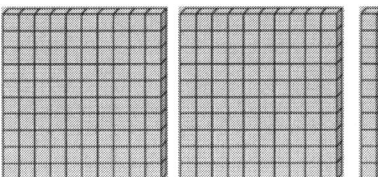

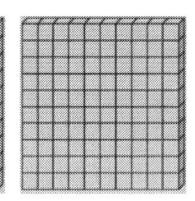

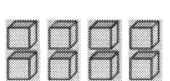

(A) 358   C 346
B 538   D 458

Common Core Standard 2.NBT.A.1 – Number & Operations in Base Ten

☐ What is the value of the underlined digit?

63<u>9</u>

A 9 tens

B 3 ones

C 9 hundreds

(D) 9 ones

Common Core Standard 2.NBT.A.1 – Number & Operations in Base Ten

☐ What is the value of the model below?

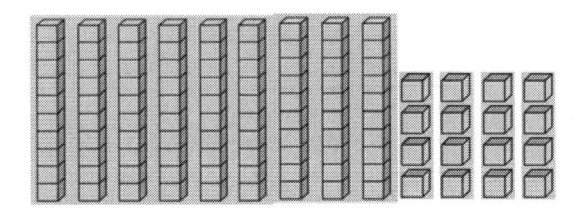

A 98   C 104
B 99   (D) 106

© Teachers' Treasures Publishing

Name _____

DIAGNOSTIC

Common Core Standard 2.NBT.A.2 – Number & Operations in Base Ten

☐ **How many flowers are there below? Count by 5s to find the correct answer.**

A 15

B 18

(C) 20

D 25

Common Core Standard 2.NBT.A.2 – Number & Operations in Base Ten

☐ **Count by 10s from 60 to 110 to fill in the blanks below.**

60 _70_ _80_ _90_ _100_ 110

(A) 70, 80, 90, 100

B 100, 90, 80, 70

C 65, 70, 75, 80, 85, 90

D 60, 80, 90, 100, 110

Common Core Standard 2.NBT.A.2 – Number & Operations in Base Ten

☐ **Count by 100s from 300 to 900 to complete the table below.**

300	400	500	600	700	800	900

A 200, 300, 400, 600, 800, 900

B 300, 400, 500, 700, 800

(C) 400, 500, 600, 700, 800

D 400, 500, 700, 800, 900

© Teachers' Treasures Publishing

Name _____

DIAGNOSTIC

Common Core Standard 2.NBT.A.2 – Number & Operations in Base Ten

☐ How many fish are there below? Count by 5s to find the answer.

A   10

(B)   15

C   20

D   25

Common Core Standard 2.NBT.A.2 – Number & Operations in Base Ten

☐ Each drawer in the dresser has 5 pairs of socks. How many pairs of socks are in 4 drawers?

A   24

B   22

C   21

(D)   20

Number of drawers	Number of pairs of socks
1	5
2	10
3	15
4	
5	25

Common Core Standard 2.NBT.A.2 – Number & Operations in Base Ten

☐ Count by 10s from 45 to 85 to fill in the blanks below.

45, _55_, _65_, _75_, 85

A   55, 60, 65, 70, 75

(B)   45, ,55, 65, 75, 85

C   45, 55, 65, 70, 85

D   45, 50, 55, 60, 65

© Teachers' Treasures Publishing

Name _____

PRACTICE

Common Core Standard 2.NBT.A.2 – Number & Operations in Base Ten

☐ How many bananas are there below? Count by 5s to find the answer.

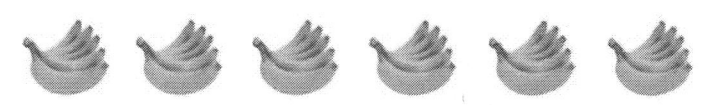

A   20   C   25
(B) 30   D   35

Common Core Standard 2.NBT.A.2 – Number & Operations in Base Ten

☐ Each box has 10 crayons. How many crayons are in 3 boxes?

Number of boxes	Number of crayons
1	10
2	20
3	

A   20   C   10
(B) 30   D   35

Common Core Standard 2.NBT.A.2 – Number & Operations in Base Ten

☐ Count by 10 from 8 to 58 to complete the table below.

| 8 | 18 | 28 | 38 | 48 | 58 |

A   28, 38, 48, 58, 68   C   8, 18, 28, 38, 40
(B) 8, 18, 28, 38, 48, 58   D   8, 18, 38, 48, 58

© Teachers' Treasures Publishing   Page 43

Name _____

PRACTICE

Common Core Standard 2.NBT.A.2 – Number & Operations in Base Ten

☐ How many flowers are there below? Count by 10s.

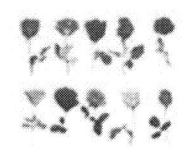

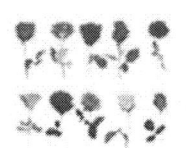

(A) 30

B 40

C 35

D 50

Common Core Standard 2.NBT.A.2 – Number & Operations in Base Ten

☐ Each fish tank has 5 fish. How many fish are in 7 tanks?

A 25

B 30

(C) 35

D 45

Number of fish tanks	Number of fish
1	5
2	10
3	15
4	20
5	25
6	30
7	35

Common Core Standard 2.NBT.A.2 – Number & Operations in Base Ten

☐ Count by 5s from 465 to 490 to complete the table below.

465	470	475	480	485	490

(A) 465, 470, 475, 480, 485, 490   C 465, 470, 475, 480

B 465, 470, 475, 480, 490   D 470, 480, 490

Name _____

PRACTICE

Common Core Standard 2.NBT.A.2 – Number & Operations in Base Ten

☐ Each shelf has 20 books. How many books are on 4 shelves?

Number of shelves	Number of books
1	20
2	40
3	60
4	

A   50

B   70

(C) 80

D   60

Common Core Standard 2.NBT.A.2 – Number & Operations in Base Ten

☐ Count by 4s to complete the table below.

27	31	35	39	43	47	51	55	59

A   27, 37, 44, 49, 56, 60

(B) 27, 35, 43, 47, 55, 59

C   27, 31, 41, 51, 61, 71

D   25, 30, 35, 40, 47, 51

Common Core Standard 2.NBT.A.2 – Number & Operations in Base Ten

☐ How many butterflies are there below? Count by 3s to find the correct answer.

A   15

B   9

C   18

(D) 12

© Teachers' Treasures Publishing

Page 45

Name _____

PRACTICE

Common Core Standard 2.NBT.A.2 – Number & Operations in Base Ten

☐ Each jar has 7 cookies. How many cookies are in 4 jars?

A 27

B 26

Ⓒ 28

D 35

Number of shelves	Number of books
1	7
2	14
3	21
4	

21
7
× 7
28

Common Core Standard 2.NBT.A.2 – Number & Operations in Base Ten

☐ Count by 6s to complete the table below.

6	12	18	24	30	36	42
48	54	60	66	72	78	84

A 12, 18, 25, 35, 48, 54, 72

Ⓒ 12, 18, 30, 36, 48, 54, 72

B 12, 24, 30, 36, 45, 55, 72

D 12, 18, 36, 42, 48, 50, 72

Common Core Standard 2.NBT.A.2 – Number & Operations in Base Ten

☐ How many seashells are there below? Count by 10s to find the correct answer.

Ⓐ 50

C 60

B 40

4D 5

© Teachers' Treasures Publishing

Name _____

ASSESSMENT

Common Core Standard 2.NBT.A.2 – Number & Operations in Base Ten

☐ There are 10 strawberries in each basket. How many strawberries are in 6 baskets?

A 66

B 50

(C) 60

D 65

Number of baskets	Number of strawberries
1	10
2	20
3	30
4	40
5	50
6	60

Common Core Standard 2.NBT.A.2 – Number & Operations in Base Ten

☐ Count by 100s from 200 to 900 to complete the table below.

| 200 | 300 | 400 | 500 | 600 | 700 | 800 | 900 |

A 100, 400, 500, 600, 900

(B) 200, 400, 600, 700, 900

C 200, 400, 500, 600, 700, 900

D 200, 300, 500, 700, 800, 900

Common Core Standard 2.NBT.A.2 – Number & Operations in Base Ten

☐ How many books are there below? Count by 5s to find the correct answer.

A 40   C 45

B 30   (D) 35

© Teachers' Treasures Publishing   Page 47

Name _____

ASSESSMENT

Common Core Standard 2.NBT.A.2 – Number & Operations in Base Ten

☐ Count by 5s from 45 to 85 to complete the table below.

| 45 | 50 | 55 | 60 | 65 | 70 | 75 | 80 | 85 |

- (A) 45, 55, 60, 70, 75, 85
- B   45, 55, 65, 75, 85
- C   55, 60, 65, 70, 80, 85
- D   45, 40, 35, 30, 25, 20

Common Core Standard 2.NBT.A.2 – Operations & Algebraic Thinking

☐ How many marbles are there below? Count by 9s to find the correct answer.

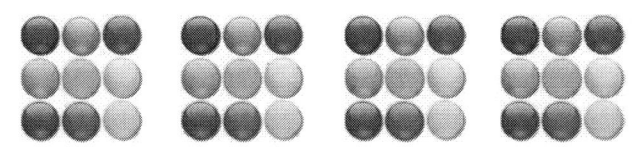

- A   18
- (B) 36
- C   27
- D   32

$$\begin{array}{r}18\\+18\\\hline 36\end{array}$$

Common Core Standard 2.NBT.A.2 – Number & Operations in Base Ten

☐ There are 10 players on each volleyball team. How many players are on 8 teams?

- A   70
- B   75
- C   90
- (D) 80

Number of teams	Number of players
1	10
2	20
3	30
4	40
5	50
6	60
7	70
8	80

© Teachers' Treasures Publishing

Name _____

DIAGNOSTIC

Common Core Standard 2.NBT.A.3 – Number & Operations in Base Ten

☐ What is the expanded form of the number 234?

    A   200 + 30 + 4

    B   200 + 300 + 4

    C   300 + 20 + 4

    D   400 + 20 + 3

Common Core Standard 2.NBT.A.3 – Number & Operations in Base Ten

☐ Find the numeral form of the number two hundred seventy-one.

    A   241

    B   721

    C   271

    D   2071

Common Core Standard 2.NBT.A.3 – Number & Operations in Base Ten

☐ Find correct answer for the problem below.

    500 + 60 + 4 = _____

    A   654

    B   564

    C   614

    D   456

© Teachers' Treasures Publishing

Name _____

DIAGNOSTIC

Common Core Standard 2.NBT.A.3 – Number & Operations in Base Ten

☐ **Write the number below in expanded form.**

249

- A   200 + 40 + 9 *(circled)*
- B   200 + 40 + 90
- C   200 + 400 + 9
- D   20 + 400 + 9

Common Core Standard 2.NBT.A.3 – Number & Operations in Base Ten

☐ **Find the correct word form for the number 586.**

- A   five hundred eighty-five
- B   five hundred eight and six
- C   five hundred eighty-six *(circled)*
- D   five thousand eighty-six

Common Core Standard 2.NBT.A.3 – Number & Operations in Base Ten

☐ **Match the expanded form to the correct place value form of the number.**

300 + 60 + 2

A

Hundreds	Tens	Ones
4	6	2

B *(circled)*

Hundreds	Tens	Ones
3	6	2

C

Hundreds	Tens	Ones
2	6	3

D

Hundreds	Tens	Ones
3	2	6

© Teachers' Treasures Publishing

Name _____

PRACTICE

Common Core Standard 2.NBT.A.3 – Number & Operations in Base Ten

☐ **Match the name of the number with its expanded form.**

Nine hundred forty - five =

- A   900 + 50 + 4
- B   900 + 40 + 4
- **C**   **900 + 40 + 5** ⟵ (circled)
- D   90 + 400 + 5

Common Core Standard 2.NBT.A.3 – Number & Operations in Base Ten

☐ **What is the expanded form of 459?**

- **A** (circled)   4 hundreds + 5 tens + 9 ones
- B   4 hundreds + 50 tens + 9 ones
- C   4 thousands + 5 tens + 9 ones
- D   4 hundred + 5 tens + 9 tens

Common Core Standard 2.NBT.A.3 – Number & Operations in Base Ten

☐ **Match the number in place value form to its expanded form.**

Hundreds	Tens	Ones
8	4	2

- A   800 + 20 + 4
- B   800 + 4 + 2
- C   80 + 40 + 2
- **D** (circled)   800 + 40 + 2

© Teachers' Treasures Publishing

Name _____

PRACTICE

Common Core Standard 2.NBT.A.3 – Number & Operations in Base Ten

☐ **Find the correct word form for number 389.**

- A   three thousand eighty-nine
- B   three hundred eight and nine
- C   three hundred eight-nine
- D   three hundred eighty-nine

Common Core Standard 2.NBT.A.3 – Number & Operations in Base Ten

☐ **Match the expanded form to the correct place value form of the number.**

$$100 + 20 + 5$$

A

Hundreds	Tens	Ones
1	2	2

C

Hundreds	Tens	Ones
1	5	2

B

Hundreds	Tens	Ones
1	2	5

D

Hundreds	Tens	Ones
2	1	5

Common Core Standard 2.NBT.A.3 – Number & Operations in Base Ten

☐ **What is the expanded form of 643?**

- A   4 hundreds + 6 tens + 3 ones
- B   6 hundreds + 40 tens + 3 ones
- C   4 thousands + 6 tens + 3 ones
- D   6 hundred + 4 tens + 3 ones

© Teachers' Treasures Publishing

Name _____

PRACTICE

Common Core Standard 2.NBT.A.3 – Number & Operations in Base Ten

☐   **Match the number in place value form to its expanded form.**

Hundreds	Tens	Ones
4	4	6

A   400 + 40 + 4

(B) 400 + 40 + 6

C   40 + 40 + 6

D   400 + 4 + 6

Common Core Standard 2.NBT.A.3 – Number & Operations in Base Ten

☐   **Match the name of the number with its expanded form.**

Seven hundred fifty - two =

A   700 + 50 + 20

B   070 + 50 + 2

(C) 700 + 50 + 2

D   70 + 500 + 2

Common Core Standard 2.NBT.A.3 – Number & Operations in Base Ten

☐   **Find the numeral form of the number one hundred ninety-three.**

A   139

B   1,039

C   1,309

(D) 193

© Teachers' Treasures Publishing

Name _____

PRACTICE

Common Core Standard 2.NBT.A.3 – Number & Operations in Base Ten

☐ **Match the expanded form to the number in place value form.**

400 + 30 + 7

A (circled)

Hundreds	Tens	Ones
4	3	7

C

Hundreds	Tens	Ones
4	7	3

B

Hundreds	Tens	Ones
3	4	7

D

Hundreds	Tens	Ones
7	3	4

Common Core Standard 2.NBT.A.3 – Number & Operations in Base Ten

☐ **What is the expanded form of 823?**

A   8 hundreds + 3 tens + 3 ones

B   8 hundreds + 20 tens + 3 ones

C   8 thousands + 2 tens + 3 ones

D   8 hundreds + 3 tens + 2 tens

Common Core Standard 2.NBT.A.3 – Number & Operations in Base Ten

☐ **Find the correct word form for number 389.**

A   three thousand eighty-nine

B   three hundred eight and nine

C   three hundred eight-nine

D (circled)   three hundred eighty-nine

© Teachers' Treasures Publishing

Name _____

ASSESSMENT

Common Core Standard 2.NBT.A.3 – Number & Operations in Base Ten

☐ Find the numeral form of the number four hundred sixty-seven.

(A) 467

B 4,067

C 4,607

D 476

Common Core Standard 2.NBT.A.3 – Number & Operations in Base Ten

☐ Match the number in place value form to its expanded form.

Thousands	Hundreds	Tens	Ones
5	6	4	8

(A) 5 thousands + 6 hundreds + 4 tens + 8 ones

B 5 thousands + 60 hundreds + 4 tens + 8 ones

C 5 thousands + 6 hundreds + 40 tens + 8 ones

D 4 thousands + 6 hundreds + 4 tens + 8 ones

Common Core Standard 2.NBT.A.3 – Number & Operations in Base Ten

☐ Match the number name with its expanded form.

Six hundred thirty - one =

A 600 + 30 + 10

B 060 + 30 + 1

C 300 + 60 + 1

(D) 600 + 30 + 1

© Teachers' Treasures Publishing

Name _____

ASSESSMENT

Common Core Standard 2.NBT.A.3 – Number & Operations in Base Ten

☐ **Find the correct word form for number 979.**

    A   nine thousand seventy-nine

    B   nine hundred seven and nine

    C   nine hundred ninety-seven

    D   nine hundred seventy-nine

Common Core Standard 2.NBT.A.3 – Number & Operations in Base Ten

☐ **Match the expanded form to the number in place value form.**

800 + 40 + 1

A

Hundreds	Tens	Ones
8	4	1

C

Hundreds	Tens	Ones
4	8	1

B

Hundreds	Tens	Ones
8	1	4

D

Hundreds	Tens	Ones
1	4	8

Common Core Standard 2.NBT.A.3 – Number & Operations in Base Ten

☐ **What is the expanded form of 6,253?**

    A   6 thousands + 5 hundreds + 2 tens + 3 ones

    B   6 thousands + 2 hundreds + 50 tens + 3 ones

    C   6 thousands + 2 hundreds + 5 tens + 3 ones

    D   6 thousands + 2 hundred + 5 tens + 2 tens

© Teachers' Treasures Publishing

Name _____

DIAGNOSTIC

Common Core Standard 2.NBT.A.4 – Number & Operations in Base Ten

☐ Which phrase makes this statement true?

23 _____ 20

A   is greater than

B   is less than

C   is equal to

D   None

Common Core Standard 2.NBT.A.4 – Number & Operations in Base Ten

☐ Compare the following numbers using > , < , = .

36 ___ 45

A   >

B   <

C   =

D   None

Common Core Standard 2.NBT.A.4 – Number & Operations in Base Ten

☐ Place the numbers in order from least to greatest.

23, 11, 35, 37, 46

A   11, 23, 35, 37, 45

B   11, 23, 37, 35, 46

C   11, 23, 35, 37, 46

D   11, 35, 37, 23, 46

© Teachers' Treasures Publishing

Name _____

DIAGNOSTIC

Common Core Standard 2.NBT.A.4 – Number & Operations in Base Ten

☐ Which phrase makes this statement true?

57 _____ 67

A   is greater than

B   is less than

C   is equal to

D   None

Common Core Standard 2.NBT.A.4 – Number & Operations in Base Ten

☐ Pick a number from the box to fill in the blank to make a true comparison.

_____ > 56

| 27, 32, 45, 55, 67, 39, 18 |

A   39

B   27

C   67

D   18

Common Core Standard 2.NBT.A.4 – Number & Operations in Base Ten

☐ Which number makes this sentence true?

36 - ____ < 30

A   5

B   6

C   7

D   2

© Teachers' Treasures Publishing

Name _____

PRACTICE

Common Core Standard 2.NBT.A.4 – Number & Operations in Base Ten

☐ Each figure is equal to 100 units. Compare the numbers below.

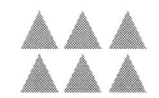

A   600 = 800

B   600 < 800

C   800 < 600

D   None

Common Core Standard 2.NBT.A.4 – Number & Operations in Base Ten

☐ A store manager monitored the number of bicycles sold every day. On which day did the store sell the most bicycles?

| Bicycles sold ||
Day	Number of bicycles
Monday	8
Tuesday	10
Wednesday	11
Thursday	9

A   Monday   C   Thursday

B   Wednesday   D   Tuesday

Common Core Standard 2.NBT.A.4 – Number & Operations in Base Ten

☐ Which phrase makes this statement true?

57 _____ 56

A   is greater than   C   is equal to

B   is less than   D   None

© Teachers' Treasures Publishing   Page 59

Name _____

PRACTICE

Common Core Standard 2.NBT.A.4 – Number & Operations in Base Ten

☐ Compare the following numbers using > , < , = .

205 ___ 215

A   >

B   <   *(circled)*

C   =

D   None

Common Core Standard 2.NBT.A.4 – Number & Operations in Base Ten

☐ Place the numbers in order from greatest to least.

94, 44, 35, 67, 28

A   28, 35, 44, 94, 67

B   28, 44, 94, 67, 35

C   28, 35, 44, 67, 94,

D   94, 67, 44, 35, 28   *(circled)*

Common Core Standard 2.NBT.A.4 – Number & Operations in Base Ten

☐ Each figure is equal to 50 units. Count the value of each unit group and compare the numbers.

A   400 = 250

B   250 < 400   *(circled)*

C   400 < 250

D   None

© Teachers' Treasures Publishing

Name _____

PRACTICE

Common Core Standard 2.NBT.A.4 – Number & Operations in Base Ten

☐ Which phrase makes this statement true?

456 _____ 564

A is greater than

B is less than

C is equal to

D None

Common Core Standard 2.NBT.A.4 – Number & Operations in Base Ten

☐ Lisa collected the outside temperature for the last 3 days. Using the chart below, find out which day had the highest temperature?

Daily Temperature	
Day	Temperature (F)
Monday	65
Tuesday	63
Wednesday	67
Thursday	66

A Monday   C Wednesday

B Thursday   D Tuesday

Common Core Standard 2.NBT.A.4 – Number & Operations in Base Ten

☐ Compare the following numbers using > , < , = .

645 ___ 654

A >

B <

C =

D None

© Teachers' Treasures Publishing

Name _____

PRACTICE

Common Core Standard 2.NBT.A.4 – Number & Operations in Base Ten

☐ Place the numbers in order from least to greatest.

450, 440, 435, 457, 448

A   435, 440, 448, 457, 450,

B   435, 440, 448, 450, 457

C   435, 440, 450, 448, 457,

D   457, 450, 448, 440, 435

Common Core Standard 2.NBT.A.4 – Number & Operations in Base Ten

☐ Each figure is equal to 100 units. Count the value of each unit group and compare the numbers.

A   1,000 = 800

B   800 < 1,000

C   1,000 < 800

D   None

Common Core Standard 2.NBT.A.4 – Number & Operations in Base Ten

☐ Which number makes this sentence true?

87 - ____ < 76

A   10

B   11

C   12

D   9

© Teachers' Treasures Publishing

Page 62

Name __June 10, 2019__

ASSESSMENT

Common Core Standard 2.NBT.A.4 – Number & Operations in Base Ten

Which phrase makes this statement true?

4,334 _____ 4,334

- A   is greater than
- B   is less than
- (C) is equal to
- D   None

Common Core Standard 2.NBT.A.4 – Number & Operations in Base Ten

Compare the following numbers using >, <, =.

565 ___ 656

- A   >
- (B) <
- C   =
- D   None

Common Core Standard 2.NBT.A.4 – Number & Operations in Base Ten

Place the numbers in order from least to greatest.

765, 432, 467, 544, 643
 5   1   2   3   4

- (A) 432, 467, 544, 643, 765
- B   432, 544, 643, 467, 765
- C   765, 643, 544, 467, 432,
- D   432, 467, 544, 765, 643

© Teachers' Treasures Publishing

Page 63

Name _____

ASSESSMENT

Common Core Standard 2.NBT.A.4 – Number & Operations in Base Ten

Pick a number from the box to fill in the blank to make a true comparison.

_____ > 128

127, 128, 125, 129, 126,

A   128   C   125
B   127   D   129 ⭕

Common Core Standard 2.NBT.A.4 – Number & Operations in Base Ten

Which number makes this sentence true?

345 - _____ < 334

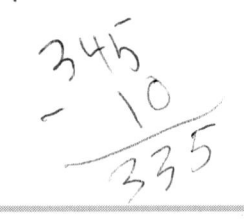

A   12 ⭕   C   10
B   9   D   8

Common Core Standard 2.NBT.A.4 – Number & Operations in Base Ten

Shalonda recorded the number of pages she read every day. Using the chart below, find out on which day did she read the most?

Pages Read	
Day	Number of pages
Monday	56
Tuesday	54
Wednesday	64
Thursday	65

A   Monday   C   Wednesday
B ⭕ Thursday   D   Tuesday

© Teachers' Treasures Publishing

Name _____

DIAGNOSTIC

Common Core Standard 2.NBT.B.5 – Number & Operations in Base Ten

☐ **Solve the addition problem below.**

$$\begin{array}{r} 44 \\ +22 \\ \hline \end{array}$$

A   76   C   65

(B)   66   D   68

Common Core Standard 2.NBT.B.5 – Number & Operations in Base Ten

☐ **Solve the addition problem below.**

$$\begin{array}{r} 34 \\ +6 \\ \hline \end{array}$$

(A)   40   C   60

B   50   D   41

Common Core Standard 2.NBT.B.5 – Number & Operations in Base Ten

☐ **Solve the subtraction problem below.**

$$\begin{array}{r} 67 \\ -10 \\ \hline 57 \end{array}$$

A   56   (C)   57

B   47   D   66

© Teachers' Treasures Publishing

Name _____

DIAGNOSTIC

Common Core Standard 2.NBT.B.5 – Number & Operations in Base Ten

☐ Solve the subtraction problem below.

$$\begin{array}{r} 37 \\ -\ 15 \\ \hline 22 \end{array}$$

(A) 22 C 20
B 12 D 32

Common Core Standard 2.NBT.B.5 – Number & Operations in Base Ten

☐ Solve the addition problem below.

$$\begin{array}{r} \overset{1}{3}4 \\ +\ 7 \\ \hline 41 \end{array}$$

A 40 C 60
B 50 (D) 41

Common Core Standard 2.NBT.B.5 – Number & Operations in Base Ten

☐ Solve the addition problem below.

$$\begin{array}{r} \overset{1}{4}2 \\ +\ 9 \\ \hline 51 \end{array}$$

A 41 C 49
B 52 (D) 51

© Teachers' Treasures Publishing

Page 66

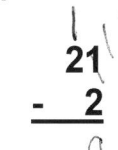

Name _____

PRACTICE

Common Core Standard 2.NBT.B.5 – Number & Operations in Base Ten

☐ **Solve the subtraction problem below.**

$$\begin{array}{r} 21 \\ -2 \\ \hline 9 \end{array}$$

A   20   (C)   19

B   23   D   9

Common Core Standard 2.NBT.B.5 – Number & Operations in Base Ten

☐ **Solve the addition problem below.**

$$\begin{array}{r} 45 \\ +45 \\ \hline 90 \end{array}$$

A   80   C   85

B   70   (D)   90

Common Core Standard 2.NBT.B.5 – Number & Operations in Base Ten

☐ **Solve the subtraction problem below.**

$$\begin{array}{r} 17 \\ -5 \\ \hline 12 \end{array}$$

(A̶)   22   C   2

(B)   12   D   10

© Teachers' Treasures Publishing

Name _____

PRACTICE

Common Core Standard 2.NBT.B.5 – Number & Operations in Base Ten

☐ **Solve the subtraction problem below.**

$$\begin{array}{r} \overset{4}{5}5 \\ -6 \\ \hline 4 \end{array}$$

A	39	C	50
(B)	49	D	36

Common Core Standard 2.NBT.B.5 – Number & Operations in Base Ten

☐ **Solve the addition problem below.**

$$\begin{array}{r} \overset{1}{2}8 \\ +8 \\ \hline 36 \end{array}$$

A	26	C	20
B	46	(D)	36

Common Core Standard 2.NBT.B.5 – Number & Operations in Base Ten

☐ **Solve the addition problem below.**

$$\begin{array}{r} 13 \\ +6 \\ \hline 19 \end{array}$$

A	20	C	18
B	7	(D)	19

© Teachers' Treasures Publishing — Page 68

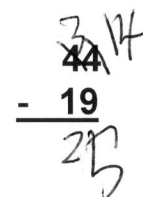

Name _____

PRACTICE

Common Core Standard 2.NBT.B.5 – Number & Operations in Base Ten

☐ **Solve the subtraction problem below.**

$$\begin{array}{r} 65 \\ -25 \\ \hline 40 \end{array}$$

A   45
B   40
C   50
D   90

Common Core Standard 2.NBT.B.5 – Number & Operations in Base Ten

☐ **Solve the subtraction problem below.**

$$\begin{array}{r} \cancel{44}^{3\,14} \\ -19 \\ \hline 25 \end{array}$$

A   25
B   35
C   63
D   15

Common Core Standard 2.NBT.B.5 – Number & Operations in Base Ten

☐ **Solve the addition problem below.**

$$\begin{array}{r} 73 \\ +14 \\ \hline 87 \end{array}$$

A   87
B   77
C   59
D   88

© Teachers' Treasures Publishing

Name _____

PRACTICE

Common Core Standard 2.NBT.B.5 – Number & Operations in Base Ten

☐ Solve the addition problem below.

$$\begin{array}{r} \overset{1}{5}3 \\ +\ 18 \\ \hline 71 \end{array}$$

(A) 71   C 35

B 81   D 61

Common Core Standard 2.NBT.B.5 – Number & Operations in Base Ten

☐ Solve the subtraction problem below.

$$\begin{array}{r} \overset{5}{\cancel{6}}\overset{16}{6} \\ -\ 18 \\ \hline 48 \end{array}$$

A 28   (C) 48

B 36   D 44

Common Core Standard 2.NBT.B.5 – Number & Operations in Base Ten

☐ Solve the addition problem below.

$$\begin{array}{r} \overset{1}{3}5 \\ +\ 27 \\ \hline 62 \end{array}$$

A 71   C 52

(B) 62   D 61

© Teachers' Treasures Publishing

Name: June 15th, 2019

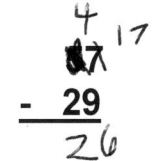

ASSESSMENT

Common Core Standard 2.NBT.B.5 – Number & Operations in Base Ten

☐ **Solve the subtraction problem below.**

$$\begin{array}{r} 78 \\ -\ 12 \\ \hline 66 \end{array}$$

A	68	Ⓒ	66
B	90	D	76

Common Core Standard 2.NBT.B.5 – Number & Operations in Base Ten

☐ **Solve the subtraction problem below.**

$$\begin{array}{r} \overset{4}{\cancel{5}}\,{}^{17} \\ -\ 29 \\ \hline 26 \end{array}$$

A	28	C	32
B	18	Ⓓ	26

Common Core Standard 2.NBT.B.5 – Number & Operations in Base Ten

☐ **Solve the addition problem below.**

$$\begin{array}{r} {}^{1}87 \\ +\ \ 4 \\ \hline 91 \end{array}$$

A	81	C	90
Ⓑ	91	D	83

Name _____

ASSESSMENT

Common Core Standard 2.NBT.B.5 – Number & Operations in Base Ten

☐ **Solve the addition problem below.**

$$\begin{array}{r} \overset{1}{2}7 \\ +27 \\ \hline 54 \end{array}$$

A   44   C   54

B   64   D   0

Common Core Standard 2.NBT.B.5 – Number & Operations in Base Ten

☐ **Solve the addition problem below.**

$$\begin{array}{r} \overset{1}{4}7 \\ +26 \\ \hline 73 \end{array}$$

A   63   C   74

B   64   D   73

Common Core Standard 2.NBT.B.5 – Number & Operations in Base Ten

☐ **Solve the subtraction problem below.**

$$\begin{array}{r} 99 \\ -15 \\ \hline 84 \end{array}$$

A   84   C   94

B   85   D   74

© Teachers' Treasures Publishing

Name _____

DIAGNOSTIC

Common Core Standard 2.NBT.B.6 – Number & Operations in Base Ten

☐ **Find the correct answer to the problem below.**

$$\begin{array}{r} \overset{1}{3}4 \\ 12 \\ +\ 19 \\ \hline 65 \end{array}$$

A   55   C   59

(B)   65   D   64

Common Core Standard 2.NBT.B.6 – Number & Operations in Base Ten

☐ **Find the correct answer to the problem below.**

$$\begin{array}{r} 77 \\ 32 \\ +\ 23 \\ \hline 22 \end{array}$$

(A)   22   C   11

B   33   D   32

Common Core Standard 2.NBT.B.6 – Number & Operations in Base Ten

☐ **Find the correct answer to the problem below.**

$$\begin{array}{r} 55 \\ 14 \\ +\ 66 \\ \hline \end{array}$$

A   121   C   136

(B)   135   D   112

© Teachers' Treasures Publishing

Name _____

DIAGNOSTIC

Common Core Standard 2.NBT.B.6 – Number & Operations in Base Ten

☐ **Find the correct answer to the problem below.**

$$\begin{array}{r} 36 \\ 10 \\ +\ 23 \\ \hline 69 \end{array}$$

- A 79
- **B 69** (circled)
- C 89
- D 59

Common Core Standard 2.NBT.B.6 – Number & Operations in Base Ten

☐ **Find the correct answer to the problem below.**

$$\begin{array}{r} 14 \\ 10 \\ 24 \\ +\ 31 \\ \hline 79 \end{array}$$

- **A 79** (circled)
- B 69
- C 89
- D 59

Common Core Standard 2.NBT.B.6 – Number & Operations in Base Ten

☐ **Find the correct answer to the problem below.**

$$\begin{array}{r} 36 \\ 43 \\ 10 \\ +\ 23 \\ \hline 112 \end{array}$$

- A 102
- B 91
- C 111
- **D 112** (circled)

© Teachers' Treasures Publishing

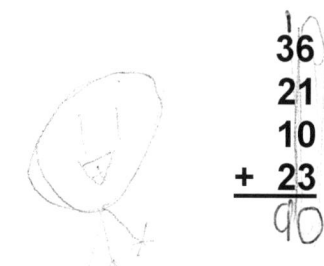

Name _____

PRACTICE

Common Core Standard 2.NBT.B.6 – Number & Operations in Base Ten

☐ **Find the correct answer to the problem below.**

$$\begin{array}{r} 36 \\ 21 \\ 10 \\ + 23 \\ \hline \end{array}$$

A 79   C 90
B 69   D 59

Common Core Standard 2.NBT.B.6 – Number & Operations in Base Ten

☐ **Find the correct answer to the problem below.**

$$\begin{array}{r} 21 \\ 43 \\ 15 \\ + 13 \\ \hline \end{array}$$

A 92   C 89
B 93   D 82

Common Core Standard 2.NBT.B.6 – Number & Operations in Base Ten

☐ **Find the correct answer to the problem below.**

$$\begin{array}{r} 32 \\ 13 \\ 20 \\ + 26 \\ \hline \end{array}$$

A 91   C 90
B 81   D 101

© Teachers' Treasures Publishing

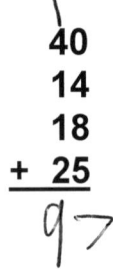

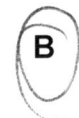

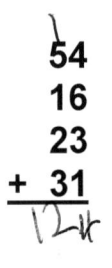

Name _____

PRACTICE

Common Core Standard 2.NBT.B.6 – Number & Operations in Base Ten

☐ **Find the correct answer to the problem below.**

```
  40
  14
  18
+ 25
```

A 98
B 97
C 96
D 87

Common Core Standard 2.NBT.B.6 – Number & Operations in Base Ten

☐ **Find the correct answer to the problem below.**

```
  54
  16
  23
+ 31
```

A 114
B 104
C 124
D 122

Common Core Standard 2.NBT.B.6 – Number & Operations in Base Ten

☐ **Find the correct answer to the problem below.**

```
  71
  15
  31
+ 44
```

A 151
B 161
C 142
D 141

© Teachers' Treasures Publishing

Page 76

Name _____

PRACTICE

Common Core Standard 2.NBT.B.6 – Number & Operations in Base Ten

☐ **Find the correct answer to the problem below.**

```
  44
  33
  20
+ 12
-----
 109
```

(A) 109   C   119

B   108   D   118

Common Core Standard 2.NBT.B.6 – Number & Operations in Base Ten

☐ **Find the correct answer to the problem below.**

```
  54
  13
  33
+ 62
-----
 162
```

A   171   (C) 162

B   151   D   172

Common Core Standard 2.NBT.B.6 – Number & Operations in Base Ten

☐ **Find the correct answer to the problem below.**

```
  27
  16
  45
+ 77
-----
 165
```

A   155   C   175

B   166   (D) 165

© Teachers' Treasures Publishing

Page 77

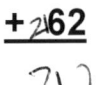

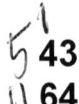

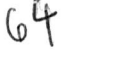

Name _____

PRACTICE

Common Core Standard 2.NBT.B.6 – Number & Operations in Base Ten

☐ **Find the correct answer to the problem below.**

$$\begin{array}{r} \overset{9}{}\overset{1}{8}2 \\ 1\,24 \\ 1\,45 \\ +\,2\,62 \\ \hline 213 \end{array}$$

(A) 213   C 223

B 224   D 123

Common Core Standard 2.NBT.B.6 – Number & Operations in Base Ten

☐ **Find the correct answer to the problem below.**

$$\begin{array}{r} \overset{5}{}\overset{1}{4}3 \\ 1\,64 \\ 1\,31 \\ +\;\;26 \\ \hline 164 \end{array}$$

A 163   (C) 164

B 166   D 174

Common Core Standard 2.NBT.B.6 – Number & Operations in Base Ten

☐ **Find the correct answer to the problem below.**

$$\begin{array}{r} \overset{8}{}\overset{1}{7}5 \\ 10\,20 \\ 1\,70 \\ +\,1\,66 \\ \hline 231 \end{array}$$

A 122   (C) 231

B 222   D 121

© Teachers' Treasures Publishing

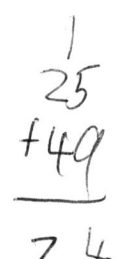

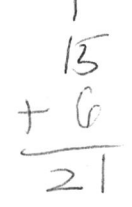

Name _____

ASSESSMENT

Common Core Standard 2.NBT.B.6 – Number & Operations in Base Ten

☐ Find the correct answer to the problem below.

```
  35
  49
  51
+ 17
```

(A) 142   C   151
B   141   D   152

Common Core Standard 2.NBT.B.6 – Number & Operations in Base Ten

☐ Find the correct answer to the problem below.

```
  87
  99
  20
+ 16
```

A   222   C   212
B   221   (D) 122

Common Core Standard 2.NBT.B.6 – Number & Operations in Base Ten

☐ Find the correct answer to the problem below.

```
  55
  71
  29
+ 46
```

A   202   (C) 201
B   211   D   301

© Teachers' Treasures Publishing   Page 79

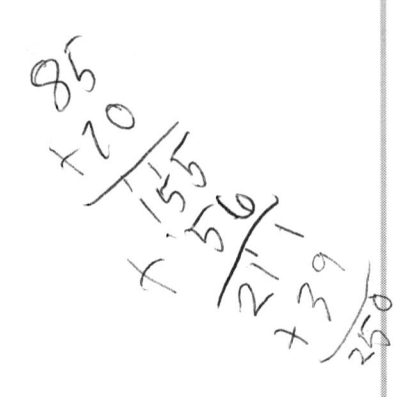

Name _____

ASSESSMENT

Common Core Standard 2.NBT.B.6 – Number & Operations in Base Ten

☐ **Find the correct answer to the problem below.**

$$\begin{array}{r} 33 \\ 18 \\ 75 \\ +\ 58 \\ \hline \end{array}$$

(A) 184   C   174

B   284   D   176

Common Core Standard 2.NBT.B.6 – Number & Operations in Base Ten

☐ **Find the correct answer to the problem below.**

$$\begin{array}{r} 88 \\ 23 \\ 60 \\ +\ 94 \\ \hline \end{array}$$

A   255   (C) 265

B   266   D   256

Common Core Standard 2.NBT.B.6 – Number & Operations in Base Ten

☐ **Find the correct answer to the problem below.**

$$\begin{array}{r} 85 \\ 70 \\ 56 \\ +\ 39 \\ \hline \end{array}$$

A   260   C   251

(B) 250   D   201

© Teachers' Treasures Publishing

Name: June 16

DIAGNOSTIC

Common Core Standard 2.NBT.B.7 – Number & Operations in Base Ten

☐ Add three-digit numbers using base ten blocks per the models below.

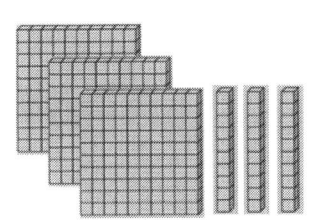

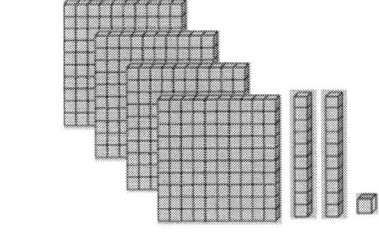

A) 651   C 655
B 750   (D) 751

Common Core Standard 2.NBT.B.7 – Number & Operations in Base Ten

☐ Find the correct answer to the problem below.

$$\begin{array}{r} 440 \\ + 126 \\ \hline 566 \end{array}$$

(A) 566   C 564
B 546   D 556

Common Core Standard 2.NBT.B.7 – Number & Operations in Base Ten

☐ Find the correct answer to the problem below.

$$\begin{array}{r} \overset{4\,10}{5\cancel{0}0} \\ - 190 \\ \hline 310 \end{array}$$

A 410   (C) 310
B 690   D 290

© Teachers' Treasures Publishing

Name _____

DIAGNOSTIC

Common Core Standard 2.NBT.B.7 – Number & Operations in Base Ten

☐ Add the numbers below. Each ☎ =100, ✂ = 10, and ▯ = 1.

☎☎☎☎☎   +   ☎☎☎
✂✂   ✂✂✂✂
▯▯▯▯   ▯▯

A   867   C   876
B   766   (D) 866

Common Core Standard 2.NBT.B.7 – Number & Operations in Base Ten

☐ Find the correct answer to the problem below.

$$\begin{array}{r}654\\-\ 233\\\hline 421\end{array}$$

(A) 421   C   321
B   431   D   556

Common Core Standard 2.NBT.B.7 – Number & Operations in Base Ten

☐ Subtract three-digit numbers using base ten blocks per the model below.

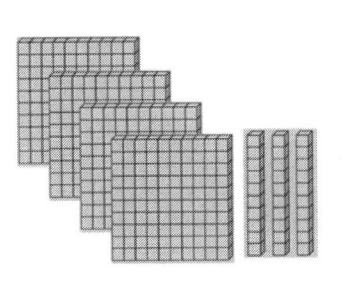

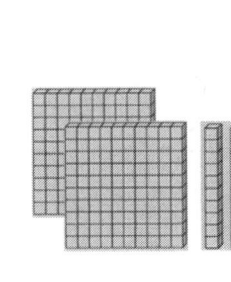

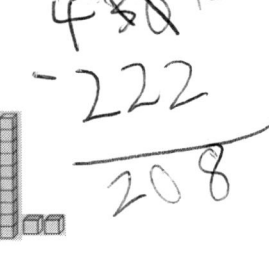

$$\begin{array}{r}4\,\overset{3}{\cancel{8}}\,\overset{10}{\cancel{0}}\\-\ 222\\\hline 208\end{array}$$

A   308   C   108
(B) 208   D   218

© Teachers' Treasures Publishing — Page 82

Name _____

PRACTICE

Common Core Standard 2.NBT.B.7 – Number & Operations in Base Ten

☐ Solve the addition problem below.

608 + 120 = _____

+120
728

A 618   C 608
B 718   (D) 728

Common Core Standard 2.NBT.B.7 – Number & Operations in Base Ten

☐ Subtract the numbers below. Each ☀ =100, ☂ = 10, and ☁ = 1.

456
☀☀☀☀   ☀☀
☂☂☂☂☂ - ☂☂☂
☁☁☁☁☁☁   ☁☁☁

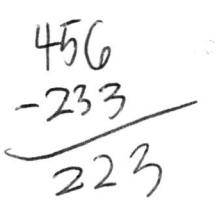

456
−233
223

(A) 223   C 323
B   232   D 233

Common Core Standard 2.NBT.B.7 – Number & Operations in Base Ten

☐ Solve the addition problem below.

  654
- 233
  421

(A) 421   C 321
B   431   D 556

© Teachers' Treasures Publishing   Page 83

Name _____

PRACTICE

Common Core Standard 2.NBT.B.7 – Number & Operations in Base Ten

☐ **Add three-digit numbers using base ten blocks per the model below.**

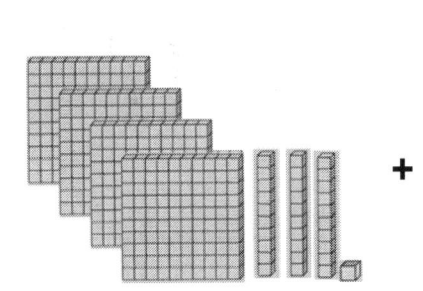

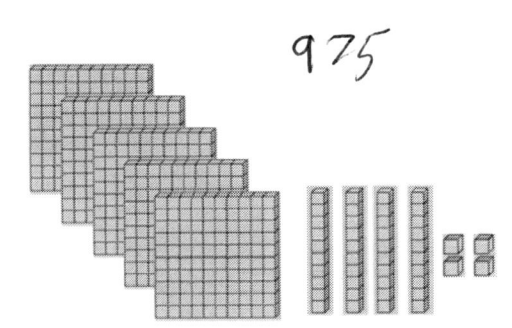

975

+

A   851   (C)   975

B   775   D   951

Common Core Standard 2.NBT.B.7 – Number & Operations in Base Ten

☐ **Solve the addition problem below.**

474 + 211 = _____

+211
―――
685

A   675   C   686

(B)   685   D   767

Common Core Standard 2.NBT.B.7 – Number & Operations in Base Ten

☐ **Find the correct answer to the problem below.**

$$\begin{array}{r} 2\,12 \\ 3\cancel{2}5 \\ -\ 233 \\ \hline 092 \end{array}$$

(A)   92   C   102

B   91   D   99

© Teachers' Treasures Publishing

Name _____

PRACTICE

Common Core Standard 2.NBT.B.7 – Number & Operations in Base Ten

☐ Add the numbers below. Each ✿ =100, ✾ = 10, and ◆ = 1.

✿✿✿✿✿
✾✾✾   +   ✿✿✿✿
◆◆◆◆◆◆◆   ✾✾✾✾
                     ◆◆◆◆◆

A   975   C   982
B   983   D   882

Common Core Standard 2.NBT.B.7 – Number & Operations in Base Ten

☐ Add three-digit numbers using base ten blocks per the model below.

582

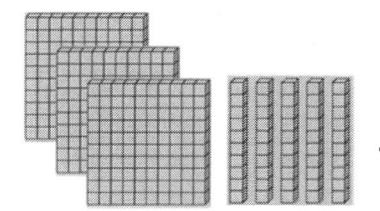

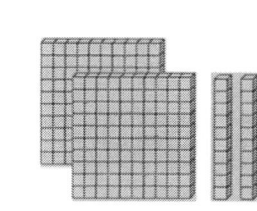

A   572   C   673
B   582   D   682

Common Core Standard 2.NBT.B.7 – Number & Operations in Base Ten

☐ Solve the addition problem below.

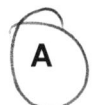

725 + 136 = _____

A   861   C   856   861
B   961   D   855

© Teachers' Treasures Publishing   Page 85

Name _____

PRACTICE

Common Core Standard 2.NBT.B.7 – Number & Operations in Base Ten

☐ Solve the addition problem below.

$$\begin{array}{r} \overset{1\,1}{268} \\ +\ 268 \\ \hline 536 \end{array}$$

A 566

B 538

C 536 *(circled)*

D 526

Common Core Standard 2.NBT.B.7 – Number & Operations in Base Ten

☐ Solve the subtraction problem below.

456 - 136 = _____

$$\begin{array}{r} -136 \\ \hline 320 \end{array}$$

A 320 *(circled)*

B 330

C 230

D 290

Common Core Standard 2.NBT.B.7 – Number & Operations in Base Ten

☐ Find the correct answer to the problem below.

$$\begin{array}{r} 990 \\ -\ 360 \\ \hline 630 \end{array}$$

A 630 *(circled)*

B 640

C 530

D 590

© Teachers' Treasures Publishing

Name _____

ASSESSMENT

Common Core Standard 2.NBT.B.7 – Number & Operations in Base Ten

☐ Solve the addition problem below.

545 + 447 = _____

A 982   C 992
B 993   D 999

Common Core Standard 2.NBT.B.7 – Number & Operations in Base Ten

☐ Add three-digit numbers using base ten blocks per the model below.

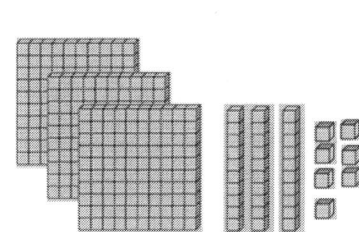

A 869   C 879
B 868   D 870

Common Core Standard 2.NBT.B.7 – Number & Operations in Base Ten

☐ Find the correct answer to the problem below.

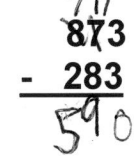

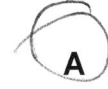

873
− 283

A 590   C 580
B 610   D 690

© Teachers' Treasures Publishing   Page 87

Name _____

ASSESSMENT

Common Core Standard 2.NBT.B.7 – Number & Operations in Base Ten

☐ Subtract the numbers. Each ⚽ =100, ⚾ = 10, and 🚲 = 1.

786 — 454   332

⚽⚽⚽⚽⚽⚽⚽   ⚽⚽⚽⚽
⚾⚾⚾⚾⚾⚾⚾⚾   —   ⚾⚾⚾⚾⚾
🚲🚲🚲🚲🚲🚲   🚲🚲🚲🚲

A   232   (C)   332
B   323   D   322

Common Core Standard 2.NBT.B.7 – Number & Operations in Base Ten

☐ **Find the correct answer to the problem below.**

$$\begin{array}{r} \overset{1\,1}{178} \\ +\ 689 \\ \hline 867 \end{array}$$

A   768   (C)   867
B   786   D   868

Common Core Standard 2.NBT.B.7 – Number & Operations in Base Ten

☐ **Solve the subtraction problem below.**

$$\overset{7\,12\,10}{820} - 155 = \underline{\qquad}$$

$$\begin{array}{r} 155 \\ \hline 675 \end{array}$$

A   665   C   655
(B) 675   D   565

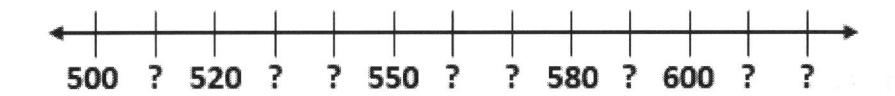

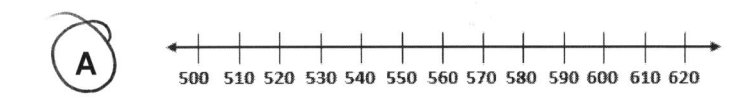

Name _____

DIAGNOSTIC

Common Core Standard 2.NBT.B.8 – Number & Operations in Base Ten

☐ Fill in the question marks to complete the number line below.

500 ? 520 ? ? 550 ? ? 580 ? 600 ? ?

(A) 500 510 520 530 540 550 560 570 580 590 600 610 620

B 500 520 530 540 550 556 560 575 580 590 599 600 620

C 500 510 520 540 545 550 564 570 580 595 600 610 620

D 500 510 520 530 540 550 565 570 580 590 600 610 620

Common Core Standard 2.NBT.B.8 – Number & Operations in Base Ten

☐ In your head add 10 to the number 146 using hundreds chart to find the correct answer below.

A   246   C   156
(B)   146   D   147

© Teachers' Treasures Publishing   Page 89

Name _____

DIAGNOSTIC

Common Core Standard 2.NBT.B.8 – Number & Operations in Base Ten

☐ Fill in the question marks to complete the number line below.

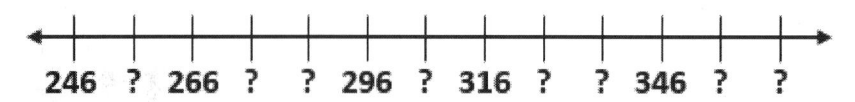

246 ? 266 ? ? 296 ? 316 ? ? 346 ? ?

(A) 246 256 266 276 286 296 306 316 326 336 346 356 366

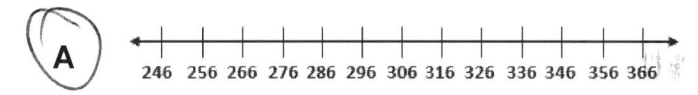

B 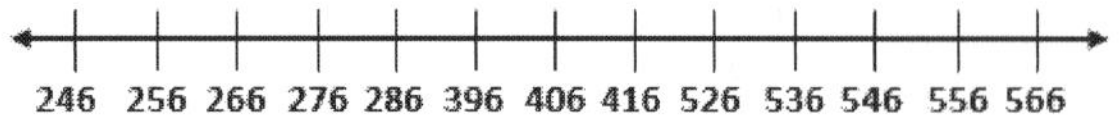   246 256 266 276 286 396 406 416 526 536 546 556 566

C 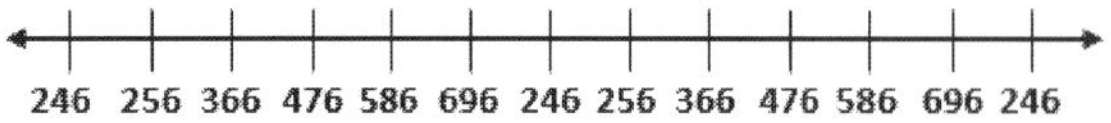   246 256 366 476 586 696 246 256 366 476 586 696 246

D   246 256 266 246 256 266 246 256 266 246 256 266 246

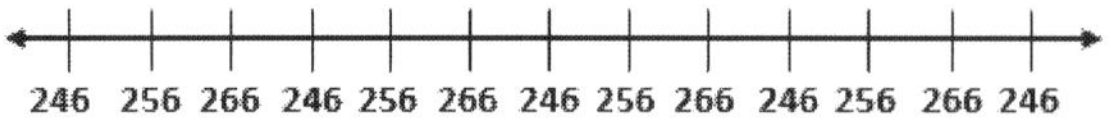

Common Core Standard 2.NBT.B.8 – Number & Operations in Base Ten

☐ Fill in the question marks to complete the number line below.

120 ? ? ? ? ? ? ? 210

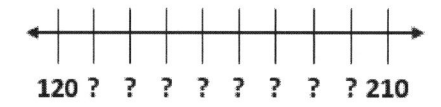

A   130, 145, 150, 170, 180, 200, 220, 230

B   130, 150, 140, 166, 170, 180, 200, 230

C   130, 140, 150, 160, 170, 180, 190, 200

(D) 120, 125, 230, 240, 250, 260, 270, 280

Common Core Standard 2.NBT.B.8 – Number & Operations in Base Ten

☐ Fill in the question marks to complete the number line below.

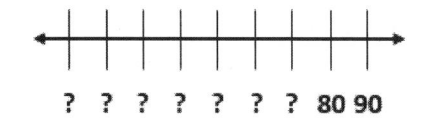

? ? ? ? ? ? ? 80 90

(A) 10, 20, 30, 40, 50, 60, 70   C   10, 22, 33, 40, 50, 60, 70

B   10, 30, 45, 50, 66, 70, 80   D   0, 10, 20, 30, 44, 50, 60, 70

© Teachers' Treasures Publishing

Page 90

Name _Mariana July 1, 20__

PRACTICE

Common Core Standard 2.NBT.B.8 – Number & Operations in Base Ten

☐ **In your head add 100 to the number 345 using base ten blocks to find the correct answer below.**

Hundreds 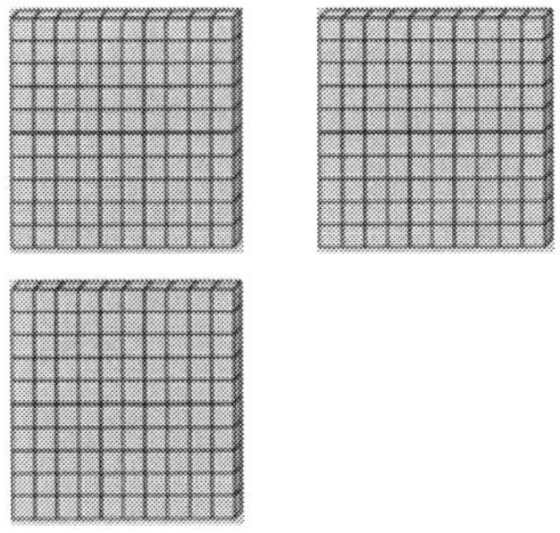	Tens 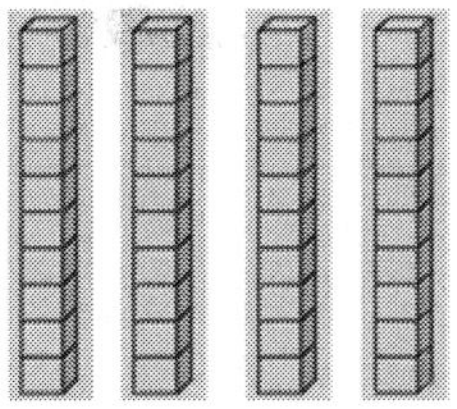	Ones 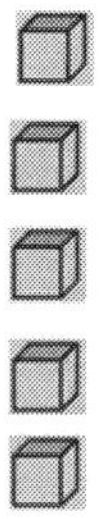

- A   445
- B   245
- C   335
- (D) 345

Common Core Standard 2.NBT.B.8 – Number & Operations in Base Ten

☐ **Fill in the question marks to complete the number line below.**

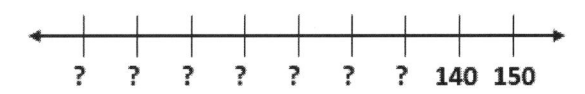

? ? ? ? ? ? ? 140 150

- A   10, 20, 30, 40, 50, 60, 70
- B   70, 75, 80, 75, 80, 85, 90
- (C) 70, 80, 90, 100, 110, 120, 130
- D   70, 80, 100, 110, 130, 140, 150

Common Core Standard 2.NBT.B.8 – Number & Operations in Base Ten

☐ **Fill in the question marks to complete the number line below.**

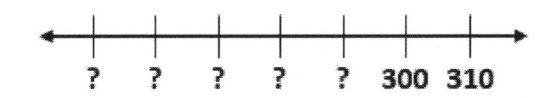

? ? ? ? ? 300 310

- A   240, 250, 270, 280, 290
- (B) 250, 260, 270, 280, 290
- C   260, 265, 270, 277, 280, 290
- D   250, 260, 240, 230, 220, 210

© Teachers' Treasures Publishing

Name _____

PRACTICE

Common Core Standard 2.NBT.B.8 – Number & Operations in Base Ten

☐ In your head subtract 10 from the number 179 using hundreds chart to find the correct answer below.

1	2	3	4	5	6	7	8	9	10
11	12	13	14	15	16	17	18	19	20
21	22	23	24	25	26	27	28	29	30
31	32	33	34	35	36	37	38	39	40
41	42	43	44	45	46	47	48	49	50
51	52	53	54	55	56	57	58	59	60
61	62	63	64	65	66	67	68	69	70
71	72	73	74	75	76	77	78	79	80
81	82	83	84	85	86	87	88	89	90
91	92	93	94	95	96	97	98	99	100

1	2	3	4	5	6	7	8	9	10
11	12	13	14	15	16	17	18	19	20
21	22	23	24	25	26	27	28	29	30
31	32	33	34	35	36	37	38	39	40
41	42	43	44	45	46	47	48	49	50
51	52	53	54	55	56	57	58	59	60
61	62	63	64	65	66	67	68	69	70
71	72	73	74	75	76	77	78	79	80
81	82	83	84	85	86	87	88	89	90
91	92	93	94	95	96	97	98	99	100

A   169   C   178

B   189   (D)   180

Common Core Standard 2.NBT.B.8 – Number & Operations in Base Ten

☐ Fill in the question marks to complete the number line below.

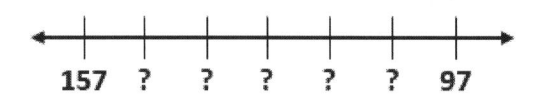

←———|———|———|———|———|———|———|———→
    157   ?   ?   ?   ?   ?   97

A   147, 137, 127, 117, 107   C   147, 156, 165, 174, 183, 192

B   147, 136, 125, 114, 103   (D)   147, 137, 117, 107, 100, 97

Common Core Standard 2.NBT.B.8 – Number & Operations in Base Ten

☐ Fill in the question marks to complete the number line below.

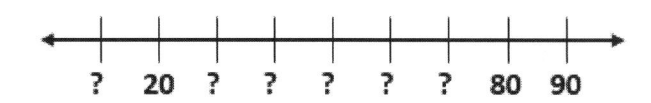

←———|———|———|———|———|———|———|———|———→
  ?   20   ?   ?   ?   ?   ?   80   90

(A)   10, 20, 30, 40, 50, 60, 70   C   0, 10, 20, 40, 50, 60, 70, 80

B   10, 20, 30, 44, 55, 66, 70   D   5, 15, 20, 35, 40, 44, 55, 60

© Teachers' Treasures Publishing

Name _____

PRACTICE

Common Core Standard 2.NBT.B.8 – Number & Operations in Base Ten

☐ In your head subtract 10 from the number 434 using base ten blocks to find the correct answer below.

Hundreds 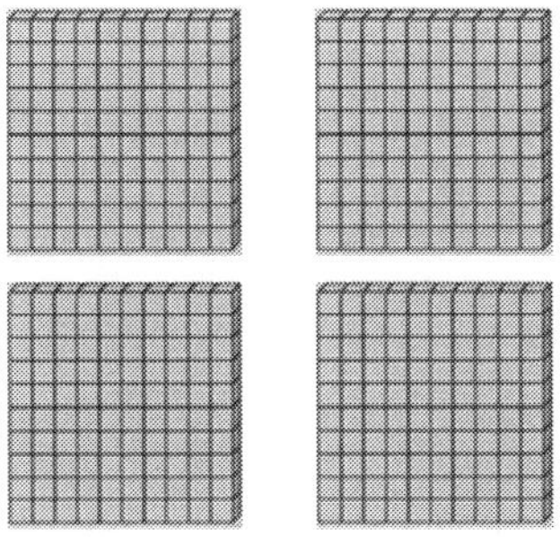	Tens 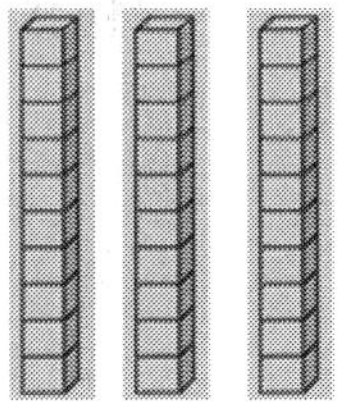	Ones 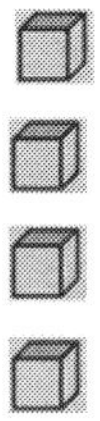

A 434   C 334

B 433   D 424

Common Core Standard 2.NBT.B.8 – Number & Operations in Base Ten

☐ Fill in the question marks to complete the number line below.

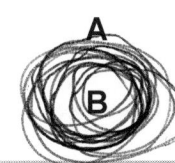

? 385 ? ? ? ? 435

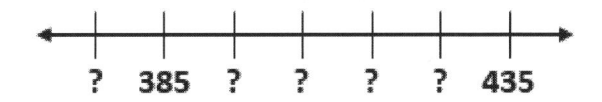

A 370, 380, 390, 425, 435   C 370, 390, 400, 410, 420

B 375, 395, 405, 415, 425   D 375, 395, 400, 410, 420

Common Core Standard 2.NBT.B.8 – Number & Operations in Base Ten

☐ Fill in the question marks to complete the number line below.

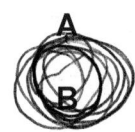

5 15 ? ? ? ? ? 75 ?

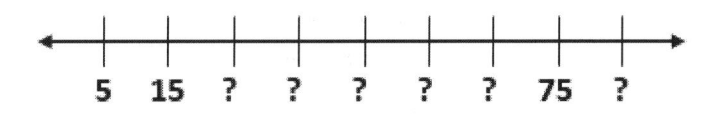

A 15, 20, 25, 35, 40, 45, 55   C 25, 26, 27, 28, 29, 30, 31

B 25, 35, 45, 55, 65, 75, 85   D 25, 40, 55, 70, 85, 100, 115

© Teachers' Treasures Publishing

Page 93

Name _____

PRACTICE

Common Core Standard 2.NBT.B.8 – Number & Operations in Base Ten

☐ In your head add 10 to the number 179 using hundreds chart to find the correct answer below.

1	2	3	4	5	6	7	8	9	10
11	12	13	14	15	16	17	18	19	20
21	22	23	24	25	26	27	28	29	30
31	32	33	34	35	36	37	38	39	40
41	42	43	44	45	46	47	48	49	50
51	52	53	54	55	56	57	58	59	60
61	62	63	64	65	66	67	68	69	70
71	72	73	74	75	76	77	78	79	80
81	82	83	84	85	86	87	88	89	90
91	92	93	94	95	96	97	98	99	100

1	2	3	4	5	6	7	8	9	10
11	12	13	14	15	16	17	18	19	20
21	22	23	24	25	26	27	28	29	30
31	32	33	34	35	36	37	38	39	40
41	42	43	44	45	46	47	48	49	50
51	52	53	54	55	56	57	58	59	60
61	62	63	64	65	66	67	68	69	70
71	72	73	74	75	76	77	78	79	80
81	82	83	84	85	86	87	88	89	90
91	92	93	94	95	96	97	98	99	100

A   189   C   178

B   169   D   180

Common Core Standard 2.NBT.B.8 – Number & Operations in Base Ten

☐ Fill in the question marks to complete the number line below.

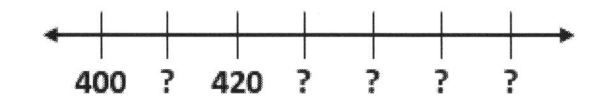

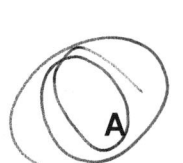

400   ?   420   ?   ?   ?   ?

A   410, 420, 430, 440, 450, 460   C   410, 400, 390, 380, 370, 360

B   400, 405, 410, 420, 435, 440   D   400, 410, 415, 425, 430, 445

Common Core Standard 2.NBT.B.8 – Number & Operations in Base Ten

☐ Fill in the question marks to complete the number line below.

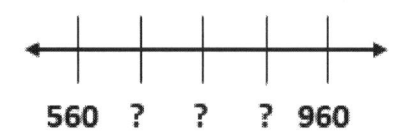

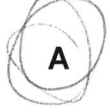

560   ?   ?   ?   960

A   560, 660, 760, 860, 960   C   540, 530, 520, 510, 500

B   560, 565, 570, 580, 590   D   560, 460, 360, 260, 160

Name _____

ASSESSMENT

Common Core Standard 2.NBT.B.8 – Number & Operations in Base Ten

☐ **In your head subtract 100 from the number 229 using base ten blocks to find the correct answer below.**

Hundreds	Tens	Ones

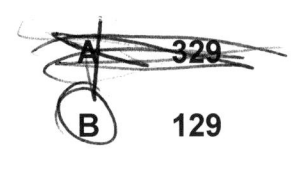

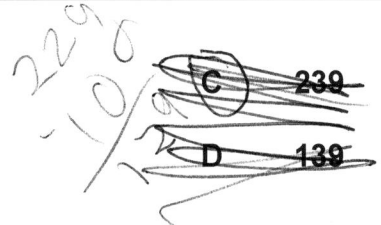

A 329

B 129

C 239

D 139

Common Core Standard 2.NBT.B.8 – Number & Operations in Base Ten

☐ **Fill in the question marks to complete the number line below.**

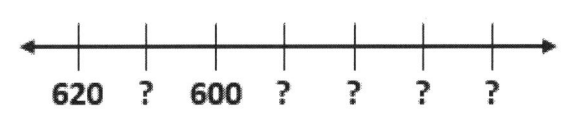

620 ? 600 ? ? ? ?

A   620, 615, 625, 635, 645, 650, 660   C   620, 615, 600, 595, 580, 575, 560

B   620, 610, 600, 590, 580, 570, 560   D   620, 630, 640, 650, 660, 670, 680

Common Core Standard 2.NBT.B.8 – Number & Operations in Base Ten

☐ **Fill in the question marks to complete the number line below.**

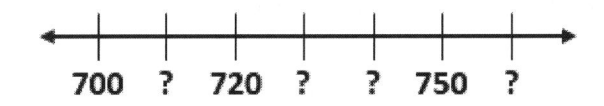

700 ? 720 ? ? 750 ?

A   710, 730, 740, 760   C   700, 750, 800, 850, 900,

B   690, 680, 670, 660   D   705, 710, 715, 720, 725

Name _____

ASSESSMENT

Common Core Standard 2.NBT.B.8 – Number & Operations in Base Ten

☐ Fill in the question marks to complete the number line below.

190 ? 210 ? ? ? ?

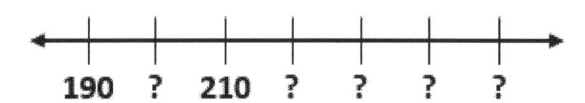

A 190, 200, 210, 220, 230, 240, 250   C 170, 180, 190, 200, 210, 220, 230

B 190, 200, 220, 230, 250, 260, 270   D 180, 185, 190, 200, 205, 215, 230

Common Core Standard 2.NBT.B.8 – Number & Operations in Base Ten

☐ Fill in the question marks to complete the number line below.

200 ? ? ? 600

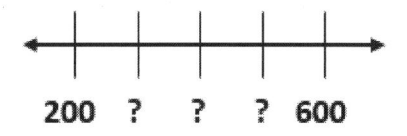

A 200, 250, 230, 350, 400   C 200, 210, 220, 230, 240

B 200, 190, 180, 170, 160   **D** 200, 300, 400, 500, 600

Common Core Standard 2.NBT.B.8 – Number & Operations in Base Ten

☐ In your head add 10 to the number 133 using hundreds chart to find the correct answer below.

A 134   C 144

B 143   D 243

© Teachers' Treasures Publishing

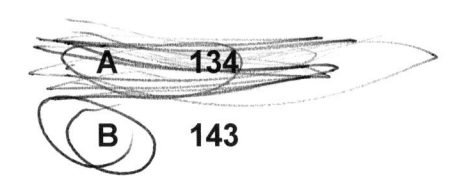

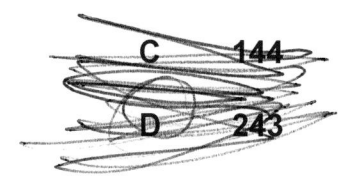

Page 96

Name _____

DIAGNOSTIC

Common Core Standard 2.NBT.B.9 – Number & Operations in Base Ten

☐ Pick the fact that does not belong in the family of 10.

　　A　　2 + 8

　　B　　9 + 1

　　C　　5 + 5

　　(D)　7 + 4

Common Core Standard 2.NBT.B.9 – Number & Operations in Base Ten

☐ Find a related addition fact for the fact family below.

15 + 5 = 20

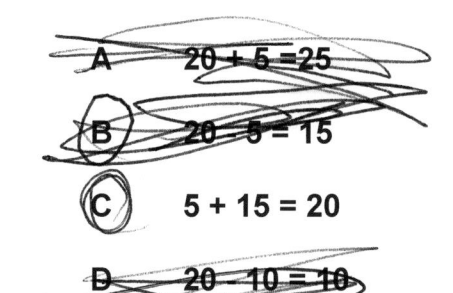

　　A　~~20 + 5 = 25~~

　　B　~~20 – 5 = 15~~

　　(C)　5 + 15 = 20

　　~~D　20 – 10 = 10~~

Common Core Standard 2.NBT.B.9 – Number & Operations in Base Ten

☐ Find a related subtraction fact for the fact family below.

18 – 7 = 11

　　(A)　18 – 11 = 7

　　B　18 + 7 = 25

　　C　7 + 11 = 18

　　D　7 + 18 = 25

Name _____

DIAGNOSTIC

Common Core Standard 2.NBT.B.9 – Number & Operations in Base Ten

☐ **Which fact is missing from this fact family?**

$$12 + 8 = 20$$

$$8 + 12 = 20$$

$$20 - 8 = 12$$

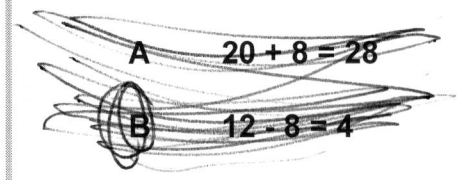

A 20 + 8 = 28 C 12 - 4 = 8

B 12 - 8 = 4 D 20 - 12 = 8

Common Core Standard 2.NBT.B.9 – Number & Operations in Base Ten

☐ **Pick the fact that does not belong in the family of 12.**

A 2 + 10

B 9 + 3

C 5 + 7

D 7 + 6

Common Core Standard 2.NBT.B.9 – Number & Operations in Base Ten

☐ **Find a related addition fact for the fact family below.**

$$12 + 9 = 21$$

A 21 + 9 = 30

B 21 - 9 = 12

C 9 + 12 = 21

D 21 - 9 = 12

© Teachers' Treasures Publishing

Page 98

Name _July 2, 2019_ PRACTICE

Common Core Standard 2.NBT.B.9 – Number & Operations in Base Ten

☐ Find the result of the addition by using a number line below.

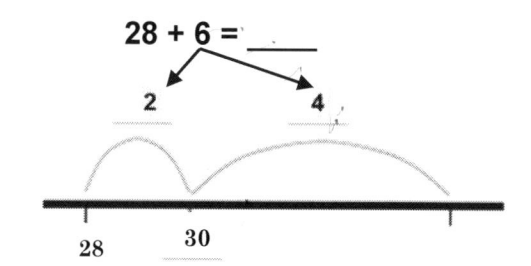

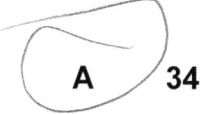

28 + 6 = ____

2   4

28   30

A 34   C 36
B 37   D 42

Common Core Standard 2.NBT.B.9 – Number & Operations in Base Ten

☐ Which fact is missing from this fact family?

25 + 6 = 31

6 + 25 = 31

31 - 6 = 25

A 25 + 8 = 33   C 31 - 25 = 6
B 25 - 6 = 19   D 31 + 25 = 56

Common Core Standard 2.NBT.B.9 – Number & Operations in Base Ten

☐ Which fact does not belong to the fact family below?

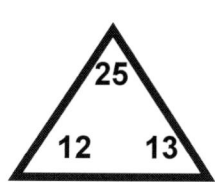

25
12 13

A 12 + 13 = 25   C 13 + 12 = 25
B 25 - 12 = 13   D 25 + 12 = 37

© Teachers' Treasures Publishing   Page 99

Name _____

PRACTICE

Common Core Standard 2.NBT.B.9 – Number & Operations in Base Ten

☐ **Find the easiest order in which to add the numbers in the box below.**

| 12   34   18 |

A   12 + 18 + 34 = 64

B   64 - 12 - 18 = 34

C   18 + 34 + 12 = 64

D   12 + 34 + 18 = 64

Common Core Standard 2.NBT.B.9 – Number & Operations in Base Ten

☐ **Find a related subtraction fact for the fact family below.**

56 - 33 = 23

A   23 + 56 = 79

B   33 + 56 = 89

C   56 - 23 = 33

D   56 - 19 = 37

Common Core Standard 2.NBT.B.9 – Number & Operations in Base Ten

☐ **Pick the fact that does not belong in the family of 34.**

A   12 + 22

B   10 + 23

C   7 + 27

D   17 + 17

Name _____

PRACTICE

Common Core Standard 2.NBT.B.9 – Number & Operations in Base Ten

☐ Which fact is missing from this fact family?

$$19 + 17 = 36$$
$$17 + 19 = 36$$
$$36 - 19 = 17$$

A 36 + 17 = 53   C 36 - 17 = 19

B 53 - 17 = 36   D 36 + 19 = 55

Common Core Standard 2.NBT.B.9 – Number & Operations in Base Ten

☐ Find the result of the addition by using a number line below.

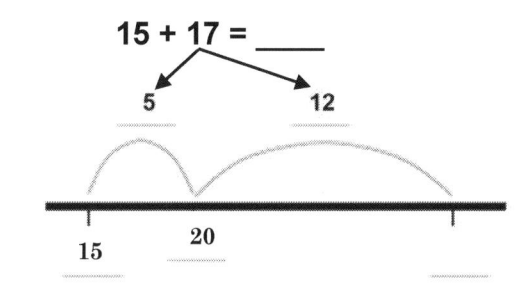

15 + 17 = ____

5 ↘ 12

15   20

A 32   C 36

B 37   D 42

Common Core Standard 2.NBT.B.9 – Number & Operations in Base Ten

☐ Which fact does not belong to the fact family below?

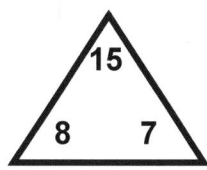

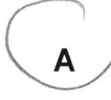

△ 15 / 8 7

A 8 + 7 = 15   C 7 + 8 = 15

B 15 - 8 = 7   D 15 + 8 = 23

© Teachers' Treasures Publishing

Page 101

Name _____

PRACTICE

Common Core Standard 2.NBT.B.9 – Number & Operations in Base Ten

☐ Find a related addition fact for the fact family below.

13 + 16 = 29

A   13 + 29 = 42

B   29 + 13 = 42

C   16 - 13 = 3

(D)   16 + 13 = 29

Common Core Standard 2.NBT.B.9 – Number & Operations in Base Ten

☐ Find the easiest order in which to add the numbers in the box below.

| 24 | 38 | 16 |

A   24 + 16 + 38 = 78

B   16 + 38 + 24 = 78

(C)   24 + 38 + 16 = 78

D   78 - 38 - 14 = 24

Common Core Standard 2.NBT.B.9 – Number & Operations in Base Ten

☐ Pick the fact that does not belong in the family of 17.

A   9 + 8

B   7 + 10

C   5 + 12

(D)   13 + 6

© Teachers' Treasures Publishing

Page 102

Name _____

ASSESSMENT

Common Core Standard 2.NBT.B.9 – Number & Operations in Base Ten

☐ **Which fact is missing from this fact family?**

$$49 + 19 = 68$$

$$19 + 49 = 68$$

$$68 - 19 = 49$$

A   68 + 19 = 87   C   68 - 49 = 19

B   87 - 49 = 38   D   68 + 49 = 117

Common Core Standard 2.NBT.B.9 – Number & Operations in Base Ten

☐ **Find the result of the addition by using a number line below.**

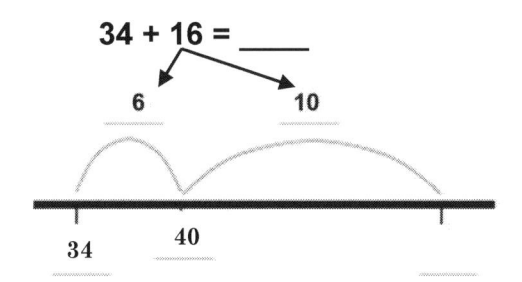

34 + 16 = _____

(number line showing 34, 40, with jumps of 6 and 10)

A   52   C   46

B   50   D   40

Common Core Standard 2.NBT.B.9 – Number & Operations in Base Ten

☐ **Which fact does not belong to the fact family below?**

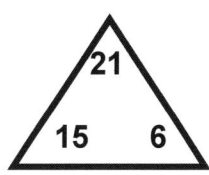

(triangle with 21 at top, 15 and 6 at bottom)

A   15 + 6 = 21   C   6 + 15 = 21

B   15 - 6 = 9   D   21 - 6 = 15

© Teachers' Treasures Publishing

Name _____

ASSESSMENT

Common Core Standard 2.NBT.B.9 – Number & Operations in Base Ten

☐ Find the easiest order in which to add the numbers in the box below.

| 13 | 54 | 27 |

(A)   13 + 54 + 27 = 94

B   94 - 13 - 54 = 27

C   13 + 27 + 54 = 94

D   27 + 54 + 13 = 94

Common Core Standard 2.NBT.B.9 – Number & Operations in Base Ten

☐ Pick the fact that does not belong in the family of 9.

A   4 + 5

B   5 + 4

(C)   3 + 7

D   6 + 3

Common Core Standard 2.NBT.B.9 – Number & Operations in Base Ten

☐ Find a related addition fact for the fact family below.

12 + 9 = 21

A   21 + 9 = 30

(B)   9 + 12 = 21

C   12 - 9 = 3

D   21 + 12 = 33

© Teachers' Treasures Publishing

Name _____

DIAGNOSTIC

Common Core Standard 2.MD.A.1 – Measurement & Data

☐ **How many full blocks does it take to measure the following object?**

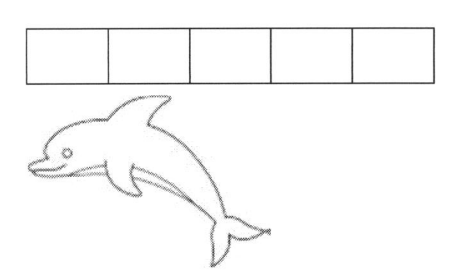

A   2 blocks   C   1 block

(B)   3 blocks   D   4 blocks

Common Core Standard 2.MD.A.1 – Measurement & Data

☐ **Which tool would you use to weigh a sack of potatoes?**

A   Clock   C   Ruler

(B)   Scale   D   Tablespoon

Common Core Standard 2.MD.A.1 – Measurement & Data

☐ **Use the ruler to measure the length of the line below.**

A   3 cm   C   2 cm

(B)   4 cm   D   5 cm

© Teachers' Treasures Publishing

Name _____

DIAGNOSTIC

Common Core Standard 2.MD.A.1 – Measurement & Data

☐ How many full blocks does it take to measure the following object?

A. 2 blocks C. 1 block
B. 3 blocks D. 4 blocks

Common Core Standard 2.MD.A.1 – Measurement & Data

☐ How many blocks tall is the following object?

A. 3 blocks C. 5 blocks
B. 2 blocks D. 4 blocks

Common Core Standard 2.MD.A.1 – Measurement & Data

☐ Which tool would you use to measure the length of a crayon?

A. Clock C. Ruler
B. Scale D. Tablespoon

© Teachers' Treasures Publishing

Page 106

Name _____

PRACTICE

Common Core Standard 2.MD.A.1 – Measurement & Data

☐ Use the ruler to measure the length of the line below.

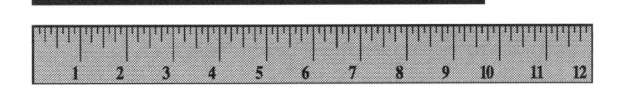

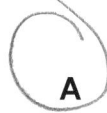

A 10 cm   C 9 cm

B 11 cm   D 8 cm

Common Core Standard 2.MD.A.1 – Measurement & Data

☐ Which tool would you use to bake brownies for the correct amount of time?

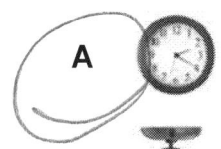

A Clock   C Calendar

B Scale   D Measuring cup

Common Core Standard 2.MD.A.1 – Measurement & Data

☐ How many full blocks does it take to measure the following object?

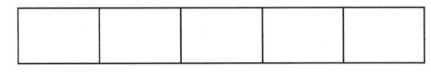

A 2 blocks   C 1 block

B 3 blocks   D 4 blocks

© Teachers' Treasures Publishing

Name _____

PRACTICE

Common Core Standard 2.MD.A.1 – Measurement & Data

☐ Which tool would you use to measure the correct amount of baking powder for the cake batter?

A Clock

C Tablespoon

B Scale

D Measuring cup

Common Core Standard 2.MD.A.1 – Measurement & Data

☐ How many blocks tall is the following object?

A 3 blocks

C 5 blocks

B 2 blocks

D 4 blocks

Common Core Standard 2.MD.A.1 – Measurement & Data

☐ Which tool would you use to measure the side of the picture frame?

A Ruler

C Tablespoon

B Scale

D Measuring cup

© Teachers' Treasures Publishing

Page 108

Name _____

PRACTICE

Common Core Standard 2.MD.A.1 – Measurement & Data

☐ **How many full blocks does it take to measure the following object?**

A	2 blocks	C	1 block
B	3 blocks	D	4 blocks

Common Core Standard 2.MD.A.1 – Measurement & Data

☐ **Which tool would you use to measure the height of a door?**

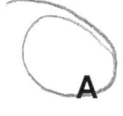

A	Measuring tape	C	Tablespoon
B	Scale	D	Measuring cup

Common Core Standard 2.MD.A.1 – Measurement & Data

☐ **Use the ruler to measure the length of the line below.**

A	7 cm	C	9 cm
B	11 cm	D	8 cm

© Teachers' Treasures Publishing

Page 109

Name _____

PRACTICE

Common Core Standard 2.MD.A.1 – Measurement & Data

☐ Which tool would you use to measure the amount of milk in a glass?

A   Measuring tape   C   Tablespoon

B   Scale   D   Measuring cup

Common Core Standard 2.MD.A.1 – Measurement & Data

☐ How many blocks tall is the following object?

A   6 blocks   C   5 blocks
B   7 blocks   D   8 blocks

Common Core Standard 2.MD.A.1 – Measurement & Data

☐ Which tool would you use to weigh the watermelon?

A   Measuring tape   C   Tablespoon

B   Scale   D   Measuring cup

© Teachers' Treasures Publishing

Name _____

ASSESSMENT

Common Core Standard 2.MD.A.1 – Measurement & Data

☐ How many full blocks does it take to measure the following object?

A   6 blocks   C   5 blocks

B   3 blocks   D   4 blocks

Common Core Standard 2.MD.A.1 – Measurement & Data

☐ Which tool would you use to measure amount of water you need to cook rice?

A   Measuring tape   C   Tablespoon

B   Scale   D   Measuring cup

Common Core Standard 2.MD.A.1 – Measurement & Data

☐ Use the ruler to measure the length of the line below.

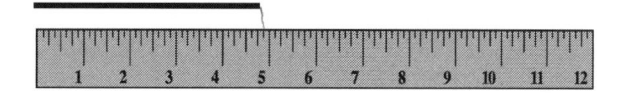

A   7 cm   C   6 cm

B   4 cm   D   5 cm

© Teachers' Treasures Publishing

Name _____

ASSESSMENT

Common Core Standard 2.MD.A.1 – Measurement & Data

☐ Which tool would you use to find out how long it will take to run from one end of a gym to the other?

A   Measuring tape   C   Stopwatch

B   Scale   D   Measuring cup

Common Core Standard 2.MD.A.1 – Measurement & Data

☐ How many blocks tall is the following object?

A   6 blocks   C   5 blocks

B   7 blocks   D   8 blocks

Common Core Standard 2.MD.A.1 – Measurement & Data

☐ Which tool would you use to find out how tall a dog is?

A   Yardstick   C   Stopwatch

B   Scale   D   Measuring cup

Name _____

DIAGNOSTIC

Common Core Standard 2.MD.A.2 – Measurement & Data

☐ Measure the table first using paper clips and then using connecting cubes. Record and compare your measurements. Did it take more paper clips or more connecting cubes to measure the table?

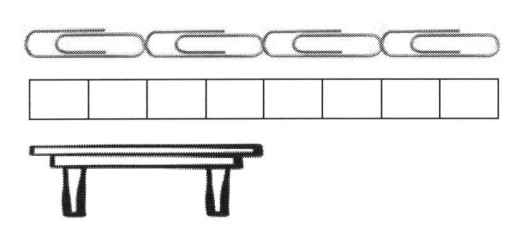

- A   It takes more paper clips.
- (B)   It takes more connecting cubes.
- C   It takes the same amount of cubes and paper clips.
- D   None of the above.

Common Core Standard 2.MD.A.2 – Measurement & Data

☐ Find the length of the object using blocks as a measurement unit.

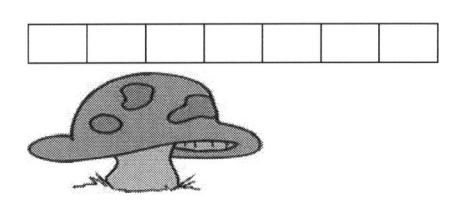

- A   3 blocks
- B   2 blocks
- C   5 blocks
- (D)   4 blocks

Common Core Standard 2.MD.A.2 – Measurement & Data

☐ If each ☐ = 1 foot, how tall is this tree?

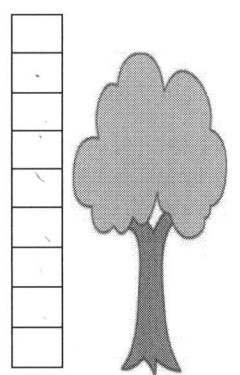

- (A)   8 feet
- B   9 feet
- C   7 feet
- D   10 feet

© Teachers' Treasures Publishing   Page 113

Name _____   DIAGNOSTIC

Common Core Standard 2.MD.A.2 – Measurement & Data

☐ Measure the baseball bat first using paper clips and then using connecting cubes. Record and compare your measurements. Did it take more paper clips or more connecting cubes to measure the bat?

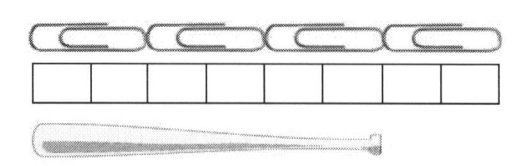

- A   It takes more paper clips.
- B   It takes more connecting cubes.
- C   It takes the same amount of cubes and paper clips.
- D   None of the above.

Common Core Standard 2.MD.A.2 – Measurement & Data

☐ Find the length of the object using blocks as a measurement unit.

- A   7 blocks
- B   6 blocks
- C   5 blocks
- D   4 blocks

Common Core Standard 2.MD.A.2 – Measurement & Data

☐ If each ☐ = 1 foot, how tall is this policeman?

- A   8 feet
- B   7 feet
- C   6 feet
- D   5 feet

© Teachers' Treasures Publishing   Page 114

Name _____

PRACTICE

Common Core Standard 2.MD.A.2 – Measurement & Data

☐ Measure the airplane first using paper clips and then using connecting cubes. Did it take more paper clips or more connecting cubes to measure the airplane?

A   It takes more paper clips.

B   It takes more connecting cubes.

C   It takes the same amount of cubes and paper clips.

D   None of the above.

Common Core Standard 2.MD.A.2 – Measurement & Data

☐ If each ☐ = 1 inch, how tall is this fishbowl?

A   8 inches

B   7 inches

C   6 inches

D   5 inches

Common Core Standard 2.MD.A.2 – Measurement & Data

☐ Find the length of the object using blocks as a measurement unit.

A   4 blocks   C   5 blocks

B   3 blocks   D   2 blocks

© Teachers' Treasures Publishing   Page 115

Name _____

PRACTICE

Common Core Standard 2.MD.A.2 – Measurement & Data

☐ If each ☐ = 1 meter, how tall is this giraffe?

A   8 meters
B   7 meters
C   6 meters
D   5 meters

Common Core Standard 2.MD.A.2 – Measurement & Data

☐ Measure the scooter first using paper clips and then using connecting cubes. Did it take more paper clips or more connecting cubes to measure the scooter?

A   It takes more paper clips.

B   It takes more connecting cubes.

C   It takes the same amount of cubes and paper clips.

D   None of the above

Common Core Standard 2.MD.A.2 – Measurement & Data

☐ Find the length of the object using blocks as a measurement unit.

A   4 blocks   C   5 blocks

B   3 blocks   D   6 blocks

© Teachers' Treasures Publishing   Page 116

Name _____

PRACTICE

Common Core Standard 2.MD.A.2 – Measurement & Data

☐ Measure the flashlight twice. First use paper clips and then use connecting cubes. Record and compare your measurements. Did it take more paper clips or more connecting cubes to measure the flashlight?

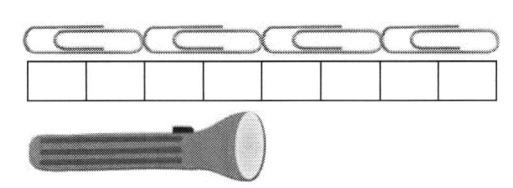

- A   It takes more paper clips.
- B   It takes more connecting cubes.
- C   It takes the same amount of cubes and paper clips.
- D   None of the above.

Common Core Standard 2.MD.A.2 – Measurement & Data

☐ Find the length of the object using blocks as a measurement unit.

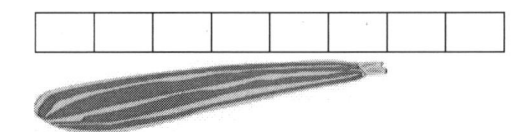

- A   6 blocks
- B   8 blocks
- C   5 blocks
- D   4 blocks

Common Core Standard 2.MD.A.2 – Measurement & Data

☐ If each ☐ = 1 centimeter, how tall is this strawberry?

- A   2 centimeters
- B   6 centimeters
- C   4 centimeters
- D   8 centimeters

© Teachers' Treasures Publishing

Name _____

PRACTICE

Common Core Standard 2.MD.A.2 – Measurement & Data

☐ If each ☐ = 1 foot, how tall is this tomato plant?

A   2 feet

B   1 foot

C   4 feet

D   3 feet

Common Core Standard 2.MD.A.2 – Measurement & Data

☐ Find the length of the hammer using blocks as a measurement unit.

A   6 blocks   C   5 blocks

B   8 blocks   D   4 blocks

Common Core Standard 2.MD.A.2 – Measurement & Data

☐ Find the length of the paper clip using blocks as a measurement unit.

A   6 blocks   C   5 blocks

B   8 blocks   D   4 blocks

© Teachers' Treasures Publishing

Name _____   ASSESSMENT

Common Core Standard 2.MD.A.2 – Measurement & Data

☐ Measure the train twice. First use paper clips and then use connecting cubes. Did it take more paper clips or more connecting cubes to measure the train?

A   It takes more paper clips.

B   It takes more connecting cubes.

C   It takes the same amount of cubes and paper clips.

D   None of the above.

Common Core Standard 2.MD.A.2 – Measurement & Data

☐ Find the length of the skillet using blocks as a measurement unit.

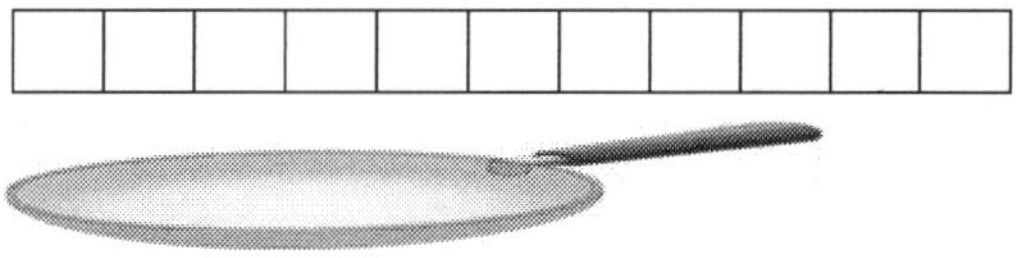

A   6 blocks   C   9 blocks

B   7 blocks   D   11 blocks

Common Core Standard 2.MD.A.2 – Measurement & Data

☐ If each ☐ = 1 inch, how tall is this bundle of grapes?

A   6 inches

B   8 inches

C   5 inches

D   10 inches

© Teachers' Treasures Publishing   Page 119

Name _____

ASSESSMENT

Common Core Standard 2.MD.A.2 – Measurement & Data

☐ Measure the boat twice. First use paper clips and then use connecting cubes. Did it take more paper clips or more connecting cubes to measure the boat?

A   It takes more paper clips.

(B) It takes more connecting cubes.

C   It takes the same amount of cubes and paper clips.

D   None of the above.

Common Core Standard 2.MD.A.2 – Measurement & Data

☐ Find the length of the object using blocks as a measurement unit.

A   6 blocks   C   5 blocks

(B) 8 blocks   D   4 blocks

Common Core Standard 2.MD.A.2 – Measurement & Data

☐ If each ☐ = 1 inch, how tall is this ice cream cone?

A   6 inches

B   8 inches

(C) 5 inches

D   10 inches

© Teachers' Treasures Publishing

Page 120

Name _____

DIAGNOSTIC

Common Core Standard 2.MD.A.3 – Measurement & Data

☐ **Estimate the lenghth of the fish from the grocery store.**

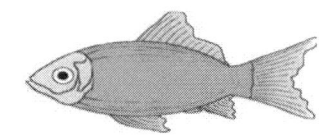

- A   10 feet
- (B)   10 meters
- C   10 inches
- D   10 yards

Common Core Standard 2.MD.A.3 – Measurement & Data

☐ **Which measuring unit is the best for estimating the height of a horse?**

- (A)   6 feet
- B   6 centimeters
- C   6 meters
- D   6 inches

Common Core Standard 2.MD.A.3 – Measurement & Data

☐ **Estimate the height of a refrigerator.**

- (A)   66 inches
- B   ~~66 meters~~
- C   66 feet
- D   ~~66 centimeters~~

© Teachers' Treasures Publishing

Page 121

Name _____

DIAGNOSTIC

Common Core Standard 2.MD.A.3 – Measurement & Data

☐ Which measuring unit is the best for estimating the length of a hair comb?

A	7 meters	C	7 feet
(B)	7 inches	D	7 centimeters

Common Core Standard 2.MD.A.3 – Measurement & Data

☐ Which is the best estimate for the length of a truck?

(A)	17 feet	C	17 meters
B	17 centimeters	D	17 inches

Common Core Standard 2.MD.A.3 – Measurement & Data

☐ Estimate the height of a chair.

(A)	33 inches	C	38 3 meters
B	33 centimeters	D	38 3 feet

© Teachers' Treasures Publishing

Page 122

Name _____

PRACTICE

Common Core Standard 2.MD.A.3 – Measurement & Data

☐ Estimate the height of a glass.

(A) 5 inches

B 5 centimeters

C 5 meters

D 5 feet

Common Core Standard 2.MD.A.3 – Measurement & Data

☐ Which is the best estimate for the weight of an apple pie?

(A) 2 pounds

B 2 tons

C 2 grams

D 2 ounces

Common Core Standard 2.MD.A.3 – Measurement & Data

☐ Which measuring unit is the best for estimating the length of an umbrella?

(A) 3 feet

B 3 meters

C 3 yards

D 3 centimeters

© Teachers' Treasures Publishing

Page 123

Name _____

PRACTICE

Common Core Standard 2.MD.A.3 – Measurement & Data

☐   Which is the best estimate for the weight of a medium size potato?

    A   4 ounces

    B   4 grams

    (C)   4 pounds

    D   4 kilograms

Common Core Standard 2.MD.A.3 – Measurement & Data

☐   Estimate the height of the door to your room.

    A   7 yards

    (B)   7 feet

    C   7 meters

    D   7 centimeters

Common Core Standard 2.MD.A.3 – Measurement & Data

☐   Estimate the length of a bunny.

    A   6 feet

    B   6 centimeters

    C   6 meters

    (D)   6 inches

© Teachers' Treasures Publishing

Name _____

PRACTICE

Common Core Standard 2.MD.A.3 – Measurement & Data

☐ Which is the best estimate for the length of a cell phone?

A 5 inches

B 5 meters

C 5 millimeters

D 5 feet

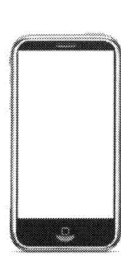

Common Core Standard 2.MD.A.3 – Measurement & Data

☐ Which measuring unit is the best for estimating the weight of a killer whale?

A 3 kilograms

B 3 tons

C 3 pounds

D 3 ounces

Common Core Standard 2.MD.A.3 – Measurement & Data

☐ Estimate the length of a large sandwich.

A 12 inches

B 12 meters

C 12 centimeters

D 12 feet

© Teachers' Treasures Publishing

Page 125

Name _____

PRACTICE

Common Core Standard 2.MD.A.3 – Measurement & Data

☐ Which is the best estimate for the length of a soccer field?

- A 105 meters
- B 105 centimeters
- (C) 105 feet
- D 105 inches

Common Core Standard 2.MD.A.3 – Measurement & Data

☐ Which measuring unit is the best for estimating the weight of a boy?

- A 48 grams
- B 48 ounces
- (C) 48 pounds
- D 48 tons

Common Core Standard 2.MD.A.3 – Measurement & Data

☐ Estimate the length of a baseball bat.

- (A) 42 centimeters
- B 42 meters
- C 42 feet
- D 42 inches

© Teachers' Treasures Publishing

Page 126

Name _____

ASSESSMENT

Common Core Standard 2.MD.A.3 – Measurement & Data

☐ Which measuring unit is the best for estimating the weight of a basketball?

    A   22 kilograms

    B   22 pounds

    C   22 grams

    (D)   22 ounces

Common Core Standard 2.MD.A.3 – Measurement & Data

☐ Estimate the length of a sea shell.

    (A)   9 centimeters

    B   9 meters

    C   9 inches

    D   9 feet

Common Core Standard 2.MD.A.3 – Measurement & Data

☐ Which is the best estimate for the length of a candle?

    (A)   4 inches

    B   4 centimeters

    C   4 meters

    D   4 feet

© Teachers' Treasures Publishing

Name _____

ASSESSMENT

Common Core Standard 2.MD.A.3 – Measurement & Data

☐ **Estimate the height of a floor lamp.**

    A   57 feet

    B   57 meters

    C   57 inches

    (D)   57 centimeters

Common Core Standard 2.MD.A.3 – Measurement & Data

☐ **Which measuring unit is the best for estimating the weight of an envelope?**

    A   6 kilograms

    B   6 grams

    (C)   6 ounces

    D   6 pounds

Common Core Standard 2.MD.A.3 – Measurement & Data

☐ **Which is the best estimate for the length of a picture frame?**

    A   16 meters

    (B)   16 centimeters

    C   16 feet

    D   16 inches

Name _____

DIAGNOSTIC

Common Core Standard 2.MD.A.4 – Measurement & Data

☐ **Measure to determine how much longer the pencil is than the paper clip.**

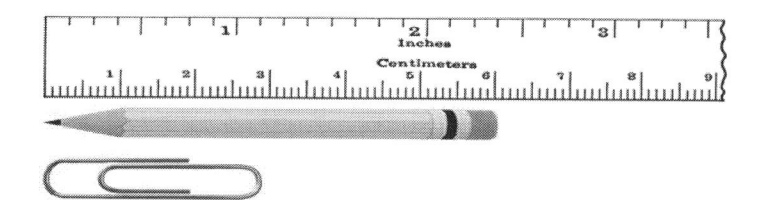

A	2 inches	C	3 inches
(B)	3 centimeters	D	2 meters

Common Core Standard 2.MD.A.4 – Measurement & Data

☐ **Measure to determine how much longer one line is than the other one.**

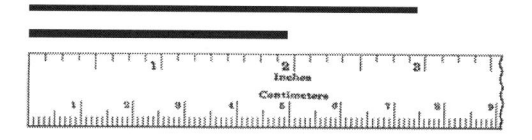

A	1 meter	C	1 inch
B	2 centimeters	(D)	2 inches

Common Core Standard 2.MD.A.4 – Measurement & Data

☐ **Using the blocks below measure the objects and determine how much longer one object is than the other. ☐ = 1 inch.**

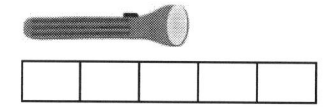

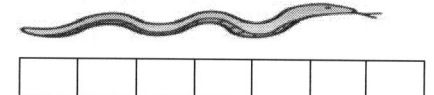

(A)	3 inches	C	2 inches
B	3 centimeters	D	4 meters

© Teachers' Treasures Publishing   Page 129

Name _____

DIAGNOSTIC

Common Core Standard 2.MD.A.4 – Measurement & Data

☐ **Measure to determine how much longer one line is than the other one.**

A	5 meter	C	4 inch
(B)	5 centimeters	D	2 inches

Common Core Standard 2.MD.A.4 – Measurement & Data

☐ **Measure to determine how much longer the pencil is than the piece of chain.**

A	1 inch	(C)	1 centimeters
B	2 centimeters	D	2 meters

Common Core Standard 2.MD.A.4 – Measurement & Data

☐ **Using the blocks below measure the objects and determine how much longer one object is than the other.** ☐ = 1 foot.

A	2 feet	C	2 inches
B	2 centimeters	(D)	1 foot

© Teachers' Treasures Publishing

Page 130

Name _____

PRACTICE

Common Core Standard 2.MD.A.4 – Measurement & Data

☐ **Measure to determine how much longer one line is than the other one.**

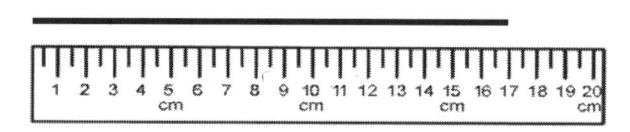

A   6 meter
B   9 centimeters
C   7 inch
D   2 feet

Common Core Standard 2.MD.A.4 – Measurement & Data

☐ **Using the blocks below measure the objects and determine how much longer one object is than the other. ☐ = 1 meter.**

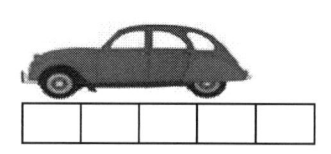

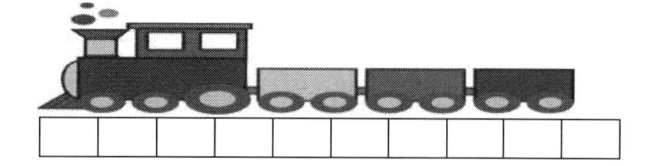

A   5 meters
B   4 centimeters
C   4 inches
D   5 feet

Common Core Standard 2.MD.A.4 – Measurement & Data

☐ **Measure to determine how much longer the piece of chain is than the paper clip.**

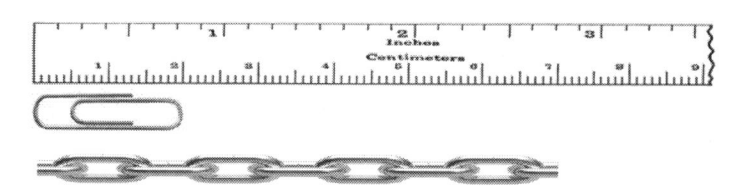

A   5 inch
B   5 centimeters
C   4 centimeters
D   4 feet

© Teachers' Treasures Publishing

Page 131

Name _____

PRACTICE

Common Core Standard 2.MD.A.4 – Measurement & Data

☐ Using the blocks below measure the objects and determine how much longer one object is than the other. ☐ = 1 foot.

A	1 meter	C	1 inches
B	6 centimeters	(D)	1 foot

Common Core Standard 2.MD.A.4 – Measurement & Data

☐ Measure to determine how much longer one line is than the other one.

A	7 meter	C	8 centimeters
(B)	7 centimeters	D	8 feet

Common Core Standard 2.MD.A.4 – Measurement & Data

☐ Using the blocks below measure the objects and determine how much longer one object is than the other. ☐ = 1 foot.

A	1 meter	C	1 inch
B	6 centimeters	(D)	1 foot

© Teachers' Treasures Publishing

Page 132

Name _____

PRACTICE

Common Core Standard 2.MD.A.4 – Measurement & Data

☐ **Using the blocks below measure the objects and determine how much longer one object is than the other.** ☐ = 2 inches.

A   1 meter

B   2 centimeters

(C)   2 inches

D   1 inch

Common Core Standard 2.MD.A.4 – Measurement & Data

☐ **Using the blocks below measure the objects and determine how much taller one object is than the other.** ☐ = 1 meter.

(A)   3 meters

B   2 meters

C   2 feet

D   3 feet

Common Core Standard 2.MD.A.4 – Measurement & Data

☐ **Measure to determine how much longer one line is than the other one.**

A   3 meter

(B)   3 centimeters

C   3 inches

D   2 inches

© Teachers' Treasures Publishing

Name _____

PRACTICE

Common Core Standard 2.MD.A.4 – Measurement & Data

☐ Using the blocks below measure the objects and determine how much longer one object is than the other. ☐ = 2 inches.

A   3 meter

B   3 centimeters

(C)   6 inches

D   3 inches

Common Core Standard 2.MD.A.4 – Measurement & Data

☐ Using the blocks below measure the objects and determine how much taller one object is than the other. ☐ = 1 inch.

A   3 meter

B   2 centimeters

C   2 feet

(D)   3 inches

Common Core Standard 2.MD.A.4 – Measurement & Data

☐ **Measure to determine how much longer the Sharpie is than the piece of chain.**

A   2 inch

(B)   3 centimeters

C   4 centimeters

D   3 feet

© Teachers' Treasures Publishing

Name _____

ASSESSMENT

Common Core Standard 2.MD.A.4 – Measurement & Data

☐ **Measure two lines below to determine how much longer one line is than the other one.**

A   2 meter
B   2 centimeters
C   3 inches
(D) 2 inches

Common Core Standard 2.MD.A.4 – Measurement & Data

☐ **Using the blocks below measure the objects and determine how much taller one object is than the other.** ☐ = 1 inch.

A   3 meter
B   2 centimeters
C   4 feet
(D) 4 inches

Common Core Standard 2.MD.A.4 – Measurement & Data

☐ **Using the blocks below measure the objects and determine how much longer one object is than the other.** ☐ = 1 inch.

A   2 feet
B   3 centimeters
(C) 2 inches
D   3 inches

© Teachers' Treasures Publishing

Name _____

ASSESSMENT

Common Core Standard 2.MD.A.4 – Measurement & Data

☐ **Measure to determine how much longer one line is than the other one.**

A	5 centimeter	C	5 inch
(B)	6 centimeters	D	6 feet

Common Core Standard 2.MD.A.4 – Measurement & Data

☐ **Using the blocks below measure the objects and determine how much taller one object is than the other.** ☐ = 1 meter.

(A) 3 meters

B 2 centimeters

C 2 feet

D 3 inches

Common Core Standard 2.MD.A.4 – Measurement & Data

☐ **Measure to determine how much longer the hammer is than the sword.**

(A) 1 inch

B 2 centimeters

C 1 foot

D 1 centimeters

© Teachers' Treasures Publishing

Page 136

Name _____

DIAGNOSTIC

Common Core Standard 2.MD.B.5 – Measurement & Data

☐ The first piece of ribbon is 4 inches long and the second piece of ribbon is 2 inches longer than the first. How long is the second one?

A 6 inches

B 2 inches

C 6 centimeters

D 8 centimeters

Common Core Standard 2.MD.B.5 – Measurement & Data

☐ Lusine's Christmas tree is 7 feet tall. Andy's tree is 1 foot shorter than Lusine's. Ani's Christmas tree is 2 feet taller than Andy's. How tall is Ani's Christmas tree?

A 8 feet

B 9 feet

C 6 feet

D 7 feet

Common Core Standard 2.MD.B.5 – Measurement & Data

☐ Griffin's ice cream is 15 centimeters tall. Jack's is 5 centimeters taller. Who has the shortest ice cream and how tall is it?

A Jack, 15 centimeters

B Jack, 20 centimeters

C Griffin, 15 centimeters

D Griffin, 20 centimeters

© Teachers' Treasures Publishing

Name _____

DIAGNOSTIC

Common Core Standard 2.MD.B.5 – Measurement & Data

☐ Nora's birthday cake is 6 inches tall. Arin's birthday cake is 2 inches taller. How tall is Arin's cake?

A   6 inches

B   7 inches

C   8 inches

D   11 inches

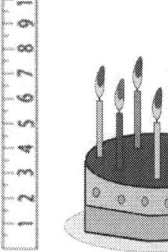

Common Core Standard 2.MD.B.5 – Measurement & Data

☐ In Andrew's backyard the oak tree is 13 feet tall. The cedar is 6 feet taller than the oak tree. The cypress tree is 4 feet shorter than the cedar tree. How many feet tall is the cypress tree?

A   15 feet

B   16 feet

C   19 feet

D   17 feet

Common Core Standard 2.MD.B.5 – Measurement & Data

☐ Mrs. Brown gave her class an art project made from blue strips of paper 25 centimeters long and red strips of paper 12 centimeters longer than the blue ones. How long were the red strips of paper?

A   25 + 12 = 37 cm

B   25 + 12 = 36 cm

C   25 - 12 = 13 cm

D   25 - 12 = 14 cm

© Teachers' Treasures Publishing

Name _____

PRACTICE

Common Core Standard 2.MD.B.5 – Measurement & Data

☐ Allontae and her friend Tashard are flying kites. Tashard's kite is 18 inches long. Allontae's is 15 inches long. Which kite is shorter and by how many inches?

A   Tashard's kite, by 3 inches

B   Allonte's kite, by 2 inches

C   Tashard's kite, by 4 inches

D   Allonte's kite, by 3 inches

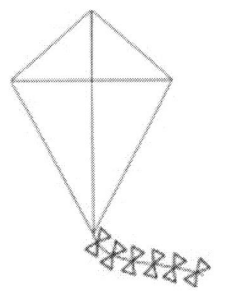

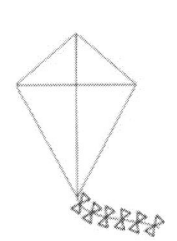

Common Core Standard 2.MD.B.5 – Measurement & Data

☐ Maria's doll is 28 centimeters tall. Ziva's doll is 10 centimeters taller than Maria's. Olivia's doll is 6 centimeters shorter than Ziva's. Which doll is shorter than 30 centimeters?

A   Maria's doll

B   Ziva's doll

C   Olivia's doll

D   None of the above.

Common Core Standard 2.MD.B.5 – Measurement & Data

☐ Drew is 3 feet tall. Mathew is 1 foot taller. How tall is Mathew?

A   2 feet

B   4 feet

C   5 feet

D   3 feet

© Teachers' Treasures Publishing

Name _____

PRACTICE

Common Core Standard 2.MD.B.5 – Measurement & Data

☐ The fence in Brendon's backyard is 8 feet tall. Nick's fence is 2 feet shorter than Brendon's. Colt's fence is 1 foot taller than Nick's fence. Whose fence is the tallest?

- (A) Brendon's fence
- B Nick's fence
- C Colt's fence
- D None of the above.

Common Core Standard 2.MD.B.5 – Measurement & Data

☐ Shadi's yellow beaded necklace is 18 inches long. Her seashell necklace is 11 inches longer. How long is Shadi's seashell necklace?

- A 19 inches
- B 28 inches
- C 30 inches
- (D) 29 inches

Common Core Standard 2.MD.B.5 – Measurement & Data

☐ Henry's robot is 13 centimeters tall. Tom's robot is 3 centimeters taller than Henry's. Bob's is 5 centimeters shorter than Tom's. Whose robot is the shortest?

- A Henry's robot
- (B) Bob's robot
- C Tom's robot
- D None of the above.

© Teachers' Treasures Publishing

Name _____

PRACTICE

Common Core Standard 2.MD.B.5 – Measurement & Data

☐ **Timothy's toy sword is 5 inches long. Alex's is 2 inches longer. How long is Alex's toy sword?**

   A   6 inches

   (B) 7 inches

   C   5 inches

   D   4 inches

Common Core Standard 2.MD.B.5 – Measurement & Data

☐ **Clair's dog is 22 inches tall. Lexi's dog is 9 inches taller. Crystal's dog is 2 inches shorter than Lexi's. Which dog is 29 inches tall?**

   A   Crystal's dog

   B   Clair's dog

   C   Lexi's dog

   (D) None of the above

Common Core Standard 2.MD.B.5 – Measurement & Data

☐ **Sam and David went fishing. Sam caught a fish that is 6 inches long. David caught a fish that is 2 inches longer. How long is David's fish?**

   (A) 8 inches

   B   7 inches

   C   4 inches

   D   2 inches

© Teachers' Treasures Publishing

Name _____

PRACTICE

Common Core Standard 2.MD.B.5 – Measurement & Data

☐ Chloe's backpack is 38 inches long. Natalie's backpack is 6 inches shorter. Daniela's is 7 inches taller than Natalie's. Which backpack is the shortest?

   A   Chloe's backpack

   (B)   Natalie's backpack

   C   Daniela's backpack

   D   None of the above

Common Core Standard 2.MD.B.5 – Measurement & Data

☐ Rosita's tooth brush is 7 inches long. Her brother's tooth brush is 3 inches longer. How long is Rosita's brother's tooth brush?

   A   4 inches

   B   9 inches

   C   8 inches

   (D)   10 inches

Common Core Standard 2.MD.B.5 – Measurement & Data

☐ A peach tree in Levon's garden is 13 feet tall. The apple tree is 5 feet taller than the peach tree. The apricot tree is 3 feet shorter than the apple tree. Which tree is the tallest and how tall is it?

   (A)   peach tree, 18 feet

   B   apple tree, 18 feet

   C   apricot tree, 20 feet

   D   apple tree, 19 feet

© Teachers' Treasures Publishing

Page 142

Name: Mariana ♡ Mariana

ASSESSMENT

Common Core Standard 2.MD.B.5 – Measurement & Data

☐ Grant's fire truck is 15 inches long. Gary's fire truck is 4 inches shorter than Grant's. Gavin's fire truck is 5 inches longer than Gary's. Who has the longest fire truck?

- A Gary
- B Grant
- **(C) Gavin**
- D None of the above

Common Core Standard 2.MD.B.5 – Measurement & Data

☐ Sakeem's truck is 9 inches long. His racecar is 3 inches shorter than his truck. How long is Sakeem's racecar?

- A 12 inches
- B 11 inches
- C 7 inches
- **(D) 6 inches**

Common Core Standard 2.MD.B.5 – Measurement & Data

☐ Nadia's grapes are 30 centimeters long. Grace's grapes are 12 centimeters shorter. How long are Grace's grapes?

- A 19 centimeters
- **(B) 18 centimeters**
- C 10 centimeters
- D 13 centimeters

```
  2 10
  3̷0̷
 -12
 ----
   18
```

© Teachers' Treasures Publishing

Page 143

Name _____

ASSESSMENT

Common Core Standard 2.MD.B.5 – Measurement & Data

☐ Bills boots are 9 inches long. Adam's boots are 3 inches longer than Bill's. Jose's boots are 2 inches longer than Bill's. Which boots are 11 foot long?

- A   Chris's boot
- B   Adam's boot
- (C) Jose's boot
- D   None of the above

Common Core Standard 2.MD.B.5 – Measurement & Data

☐ Brianna's pool is 5 feet deep. Mandy's pool is 2 feet deeper. How deep is Mandy's pool?

- (A) 7 feet
- B   6 feet
- C   3 feet
- D   8 feet

Common Core Standard 2.MD.B.5 – Measurement & Data

☐ Layla's red binder is 2 inches thick. Her green binder is 1 inch thicker than the red one. Layla's white binder is 1 inch thinner than the red one. Which binder is the thickest one?

- A   red binder
- (B) green binder
- C   white binder
- D   None of the above

© Teachers' Treasures Publishing

Name _____ DIAGNOSTIC

Common Core Standard 2.MD.B.6 – Measurement & Data

☐ With the help of the number line diagram find the sum of the whole numbers.

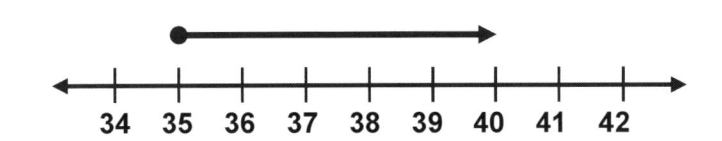

$$35 + 5 = \underline{}$$

(number line from 34 to 42, arrow from 35 to 40)

$$\begin{array}{r} \overset{1}{35} \\ +5 \\ \hline 40 \end{array}$$

A   30   C   35
(B)   40   D   39

Common Core Standard 2.MD.B.6 – Measurement & Data

☐ Write the addition equation of the whole numbers using the number line diagram.

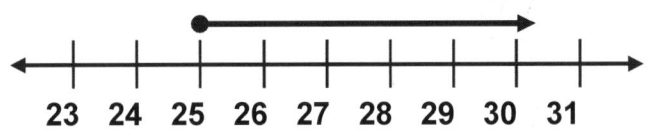

(number line from 23 to 31, arrow from 25 to 30)

(A)   25 + 5 = 30   C   24 + 5 = 29
B   30 + 5 = 35   D   25 - 5 = 20

Common Core Standard 2.MD.B.6 – Measurement & Data

☐ With the help of the number line diagram find the difference of the whole numbers.

$$50 - 4 = \underline{}$$

(number line from 44 to 50, arrow from 50 to 46)

A   64   (C)   46
B   47   D   43

© Teachers' Treasures Publishing   Page 145

Name _____

DIAGNOSTIC

Common Core Standard 2.MD.B.6 – Measurement & Data

Write the addition equation of the whole numbers using the number line diagram.

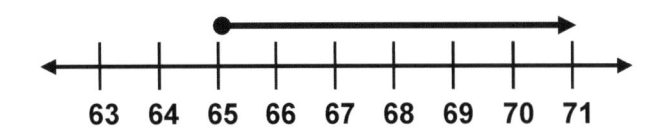

A	65 + 5 = 70	C	65 - 5 = 60
(B)	65 + 6 = 71	D	65 - 6 = 59

Common Core Standard 2.MD.B.6 – Measurement & Data

Write the addition equation of the numbers using the number line diagram.

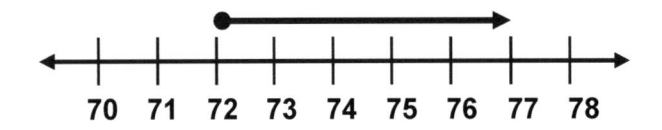

A	72 + 3 = 75	C	72 - 5 = 67
B	72 + 4 = 76	(D)	72 + 5 = 77

Common Core Standard 2.MD.B.6 – Measurement & Data

With the help of the number line diagram find the difference of the whole numbers.

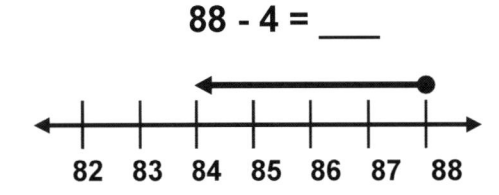

88 - 4 = ___

(A)	84	C	92
B	64	D	83

Name _____

PRACTICE

Common Core Standard 2.MD.B.6 – Measurement & Data

Write the subtraction equation of the whole numbers using the number line diagram.

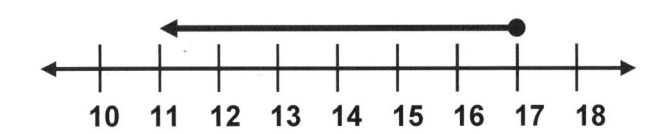

10 11 12 13 14 15 16 17 18

A   17 + 6 = 23   C   23 - 3 = 17
B   17 - 6 = 11   D   17 - 5 = 12

Common Core Standard 2.MD.B.6 – Measurement & Data

With the help of the number line diagram find the sum of the whole numbers.

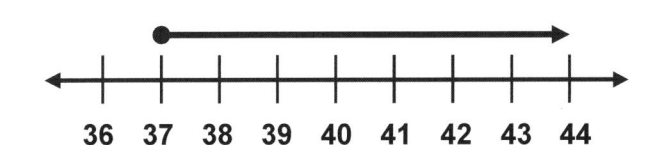

37 + 7 = ___

36 37 38 39 40 41 42 43 44

A   30   C   44
B   41   D   43

Common Core Standard 2.MD.B.6 – Measurement & Data

Write the equation of the subtraction of the numbers shown on the number line.

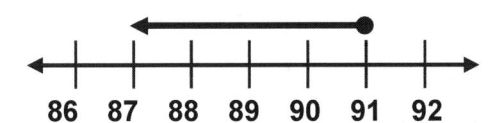

86 87 88 89 90 91 92

A   91 - 4 = 87   C   91 + 4 = 95
B   91 - 4 = 86   D   91 - 5 = 86

© Teachers' Treasures Publishing

Page 147

Name _____

PRACTICE

Common Core Standard 2.MD.B.6 – Measurement & Data

☐ **With the help of the number line diagram find the difference of the whole numbers.**

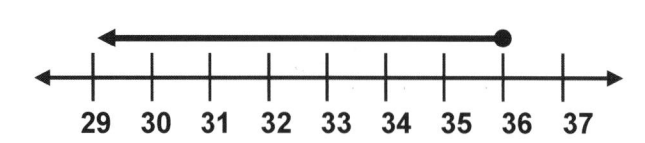

36 - 7 = ___

29 30 31 32 33 34 35 36 37

A   36   (C)   29

B   30   D   43

Common Core Standard 2.MD.B.6 – Measurement & Data

☐ **With the help of the number line diagram find the sum of the whole numbers.**

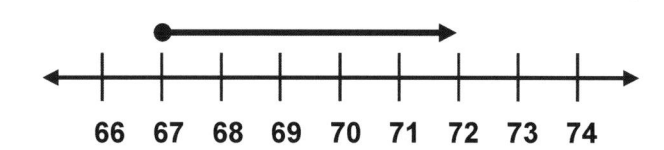

67 + 5 = ___

66 67 68 69 70 71 72 73 74

(A)   72   C   62

B   73   D   63

Common Core Standard 2.MD.B.6 – Measurement & Data

☐ **Write the equation of the addition of the numbers shown on the number line below.**

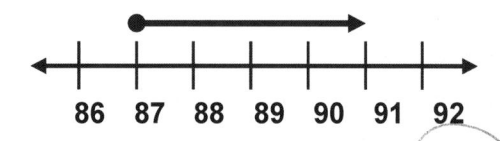

86 87 88 89 90 91 92

A   87 + 4 = 87   (C)   87 + 4 = 91

B   87 - 4 = 83   D   88 + 4 = 92

© Teachers' Treasures Publishing   Page 148

Name _____

PRACTICE

Common Core Standard 2.MD.B.6 – Measurement & Data

☐ **Write the addition equation of the numbers using the number line diagram.**

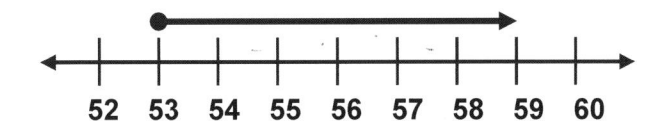

(number line from 52 to 60 with arrow from 53 to 59)

A   53 + 5 = 58   C   53 - 6 = 47

(B) 53 + 6 = 59   D   53 + 7 = 60

Common Core Standard 2.MD.B.6 – Measurement & Data

☐ **With the help of the number line diagram find the difference of the whole numbers.**

32 - 9 = ___

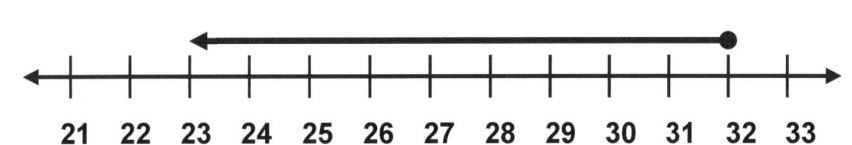

(number line from 21 to 33 with arrow from 32 back to 23)

A   22   C   24

B   41   (D) 23

Common Core Standard 2.MD.B.6 – Measurement & Data

☐ **With the help of the number line diagram find the sum of the whole numbers.**

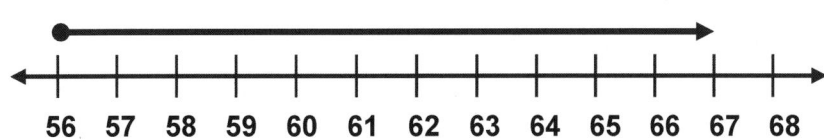

56 + 11 = ___

(number line from 56 to 68 with arrow from 56 to 67)

(A) 67   C   68

B   66   D   45

© Teachers' Treasures Publishing

Page 149

Name _____

PRACTICE

Common Core Standard 2.MD.B.6 – Measurement & Data

☐ Write the subtraction equation of the whole numbers using the number line diagram.

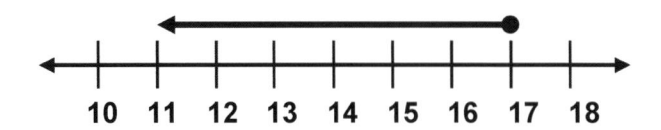

```
  ←―――――――•
├──┼──┼──┼──┼──┼──┼──┼──┤
10  11  12  13  14  15  16  17  18
```

A   17 + 6 = 23   C   23 - 3 = 17

(B)   17 - 6 = 11   D   17 - 5 = 12

Common Core Standard 2.MD.B.6 – Measurement & Data

☐ With the help of the number line diagram find the sum of the whole numbers.

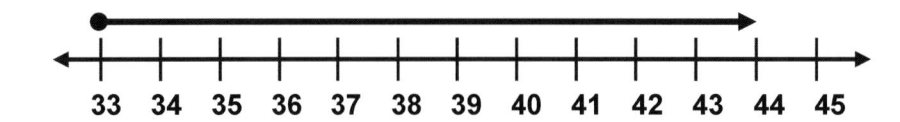

33 + 11 = ___

```
•―――――――――――――→
├──┼──┼──┼──┼──┼──┼──┼──┼──┼──┼──┤
33  34  35  36  37  38  39  40  41  42  43  44  45
```

A   55   C   54

(B)   44   D   22

Common Core Standard 2.MD.B.6 – Measurement & Data

☐ Write the subtraction equation of the numbers using the number line diagram.

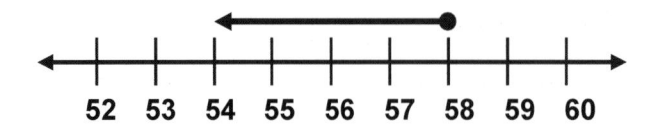

```
       ←―――――•
├──┼──┼──┼──┼──┼──┼──┼──┤
52  53  54  55  56  57  58  59  60
```

A   58 - 5 = 52   C   58 - 6 = 52

B   58 + 4 = 62   (D)   58 - 4 = 54

© Teachers' Treasures Publishing   Page 150

Name _____

ASSESSMENT

Common Core Standard 2.MD.B.6 – Measurement & Data

☐ **Write the subtraction equation of the whole numbers using the number line diagram.**

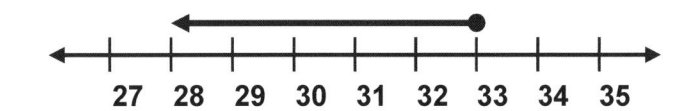

27 28 29 30 31 32 33 34 35

(A) 33 - 5 = 28   C   33 - 6 = 27
B   33 - 5 = 27   D   33 + 5 = 38

Common Core Standard 2.MD.B.6 – Measurement & Data

☐ **With the help of the number line diagram find the sum of the whole numbers.**

64 + 7 = ___

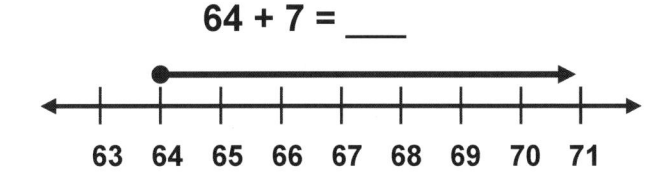

63 64 65 66 67 68 69 70 71

A   70   C   72
B   73   (D) 71

Common Core Standard 2.MD.B.6 – Measurement & Data

☐ **With the help of the number line diagram find the sum of the whole numbers.**

19 + 9 = ___

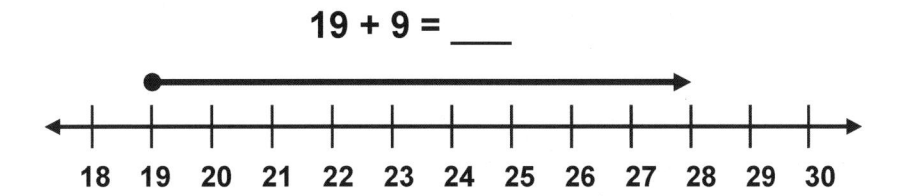

18 19 20 21 22 23 24 25 26 27 28 29 30

A   27   C   38
(B) 28   D   18

© Teachers' Treasures Publishing   Page 151

Name _____

ASSESSMENT

Common Core Standard 2.MD.B.6 – Measurement & Data

☐ **With the help of the number line diagram find the difference of the whole numbers.**

28 - 7 = ___

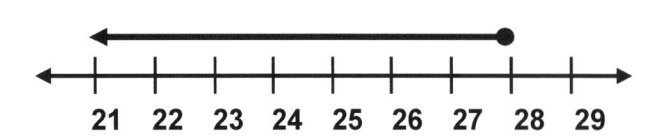

| A | 22 | C | 24 |
| B | 21 | D | 23 |

(B is circled)

Common Core Standard 2.MD.B.6 – Measurement & Data

☐ **Write the subtraction equation of the numbers using the number line diagram.**

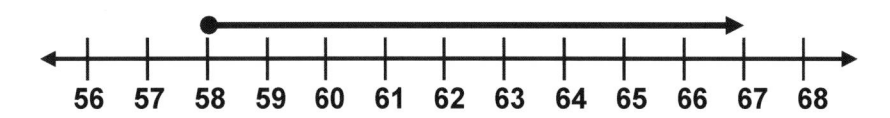

| A | 58 + 9 = 66 | C | 58 + 9 = 67 |
| B | 58 - 9 = 49 | D | 58 + 9 = 68 |

(C is circled)

Common Core Standard 2.MD.B.6 – Measurement & Data

☐ **With the help of the number line diagram find the sum of the whole numbers.**

39 + 5 = ___

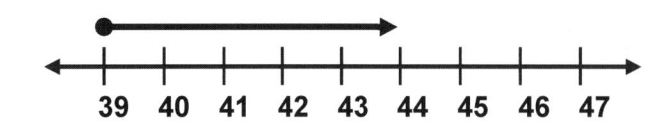

| A | 42 | C | 44 |
| B | 43 | D | 45 |

(C is circled)

© Teachers' Treasures Publishing

Page 152

Name _____

DIAGNOSTIC

Common Core Standard 2.MD.C.7 – Measurement & Data

☐ What time does the clock below show?

A   2:00

(B)   3:00

C   4:00

D   12:00

Common Core Standard 2.MD.C.7 – Measurement & Data

☐ Which clock shows the same time as the digital clock below?

1:30

A

B

C

(D)

Common Core Standard 2.MD.C.7 – Measurement & Data

☐ What time does the clock below show?

A   eight o'clock

B   twelve o'clock

(C)   nine o'clock

D   ten o'clock

© Teachers' Treasures Publishing

Name _____

DIAGNOSTIC

Common Core Standard 2.MD.C.7 – Measurement & Data

☐ Which digital clock shows five o'clock?

A 7:00

(C) 5:00

B 6:00

D 4:00

Common Core Standard 2.MD.C.7 – Measurement & Data

☐ How many days are in one week?

A   24 days

B   14 days

(C) 7 days

D   30 days

Common Core Standard 2.MD.C.7 – Measurement & Data

☐ Find the missing time in the pattern.

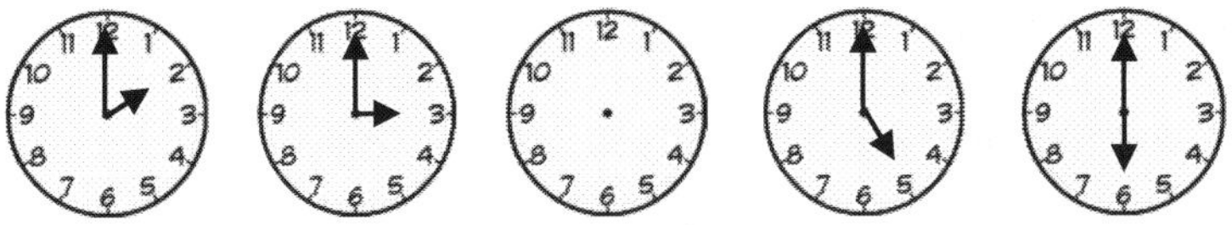

A

B

C

(D)

Page 154

Name _____

PRACTICE

Common Core Standard 2.MD.C.7 – Measurement & Data

☐ What time is shown on the clock below?

- (A) two o'clock
- C one o'clock
- B twelve o'clock
- D eleven o'clock

Common Core Standard 2.MD.C.7 – Measurement & Data

☐ Anna goes to dance in the afternoon. Find what time her dance starts from the clock below including a.m. or p. m.

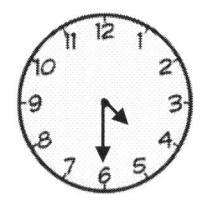

- A   3:30 a.m.
- (C)   4:30 p.m.
- B   4:30 a.m.
- D   3:30 p.m.

Common Core Standard 2.MD.A.C.7 – Measurement & Data

☐ Which digital clock shows half past three o'clock?

- (A) 3:30
- C   3:20
- B   3:15
- D   3:45

© Teachers' Treasures Publishing

Page 155

Name _____

PRACTICE

Common Core Standard 2.MD.C.7 – Measurement & Data

☐ Which month comes right before February?

- (A) March
- B December
- C January
- D November

Common Core Standard 2.MD.C.7 – Measurement & Data

☐ Find the missing time in the pattern.

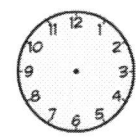

A
B
C
(D)

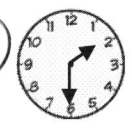

Common Core Standard 2.MD.C.7 – Measurement & Data

☐ What time does the digital clock below show?

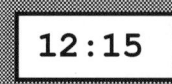

12:15

- A quarter after twelve o'clock
- B quarter before one o'clock
- (C) half past twelve o'clock
- D half past eleven o'clock

© Teachers' Treasures Publishing

Page 156

Name _____

PRACTICE

Common Core Standard 2.MD.C.7 – Measurement & Data

Jason's band practice starts at 4:00 p.m. and lasts for two hours. What time does his practice end?

A   6:00 a.m.

B   5:00 p.m.

C   6:30 p.m.

D   6:00 p.m.

Common Core Standard 2.MD.C.7 – Measurement & Data

Which digital clock shows the same time as the clock below?

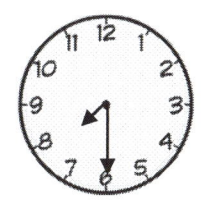

A   8:30

B   7:45

C   7:30

D   6:40

Common Core Standard 2.MD.C.7 – Measurement & Data

Tomorrow is Wednesday. What day was yesterday?

A   Tuesday

B   Monday

C   Thursday

D   Friday

© Teachers' Treasures Publishing

Name _____

PRACTICE

Common Core Standard 2.MD.C.7 – Measurement & Data

☐ What time does the clock below show?

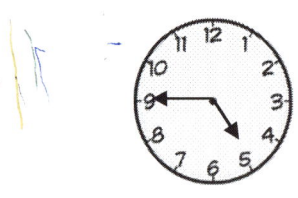

A   quarter before five o'clock

B   quarter before four o'clock

C   quarter after nine o'clock

D   halve past four o'clock

Common Core Standard 2.MD.C.7 – Measurement & Data

☐ Sally's volleyball practice starts in the morning. Find what time her practice starts from the clock below including a.m. or p.m.

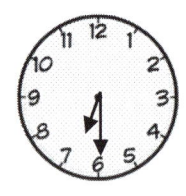

A   6:30 a.m.   C   8:30 a.m.

B   7:30 p.m.   D   6:30 p.m.

Common Core Standard 2.MD.C.7 – Measurement & Data

☐ What time does the digital clock below show?

9:45

A   quarter after nine o'clock

B   quarter after ten o'clock

C   quarter before ten o'clock

D   quarter before nine o'clock

© Teachers' Treasures Publishing

Name _____

ASSESSMENT

Common Core Standard 2.MD.C.7 – Measurement & Data

☐ Find the missing time in the pattern.

A

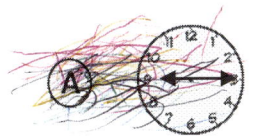

B

D

Common Core Standard 2.MD.C.7 – Measurement & Data

☐ Which digital clock shows the same time as the clock below?

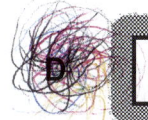

A 5:30

B 3:45

C 4:15

D 5:15

Common Core Standard 2.MD.C.7 – Measurement & Data

☐ What is the date of second Monday of June?

A   June 11
B   June 12
C   June 19
D   June 26

June						
Sun	Mon	Tue	Wed	Thu	Fri	Sat
				1	2	3
4	5	6	7	8	9	10
11	12	13	14	15	16	17
18	19	20	21	22	23	24
25	26	27	28	29	30	

© Teachers' Treasures Publishing

Page 159

Name _____

ASSESSMENT

Common Core Standard 2.MD.C.7 – Measurement & Data

☐   Arsema's theater performance started at 6:00 p.m. and lasted three hours. What time did the performance end?

A   8:00 a.m.

B   9:00 p.m.

C   8:30 p.m.

D   7:00 p.m.

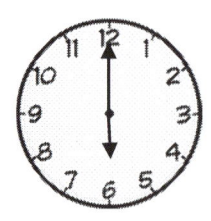

Common Core Standard 2.MD.C.7 – Measurement & Data

☐   What time does the digital clock below show?

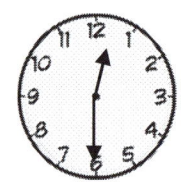

A   half past one o'clock

B   quarter before twelve o'clock

C   half past twelve o'clock

D   halve past eleven o'clock

Common Core Standard 2.MD.C.7 – Measurement & Data

☐   How many days are in the month of March?

A   28

B   29

C   30

D   31

© Teachers' Treasures Publishing

Page 160

Name _____

DIAGNOSTIC

Common Core Standard 2.MD.C.8 – Measurement & Data

☐ Jake has 3 quarters and 5 pennies. How many cents does he have?

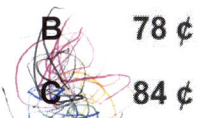

A   80 ¢
B   78 ¢
C   84 ¢
D   85 ¢

Common Core Standard 2.MD.C.8 – Measurement & Data

☐ Which is not equal to ten dimes?

A   two quarters, four dimes, two nickels
B   one quarter, seven dimes, five pennies
C   three quarters, two dimes, one nickel
D   two quarters, four dimes, three nickels

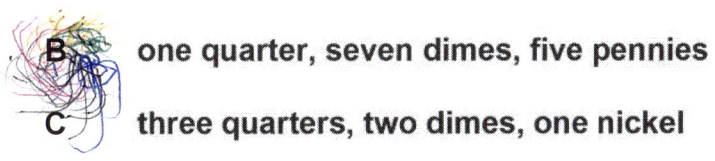

Common Core Standard 2.MD.C.8 – Measurement & Data

☐ Look at the coins in the box. Which group of coins shows the same amount?

A 
B 
C 
D

© Teachers' Treasures Publishing   Page 161

Name _____

DIAGNOSTIC

Common Core Standard 2.MD.C.8 – Measurement & Data

☐ **Nathan spent four dimes on an eraser. Dominic spent a quarter on a sharpener. How much did they spend in all?**

A   45 ¢

B   65¢

C   60¢

D   55 ¢

Common Core Standard 2.MD.C.8 – Measurement & Data

☐ **Lara buys a box of colored pencils for 48¢. She pays the cashier with a one dollar bill. The cashier gives her change back by using the least amount of coins. Which coins does Lara receive?**

A   two quarters and two pennies

B   one quarter, two dimes, one nickel

C   one quarter, one dime, one nickel, five pennies

D   one quarter, two dimes, one nickel, one penny

Common Core Standard 2.MD.C.8 – Measurement & Data

☐ **How much are the coins below worth?**

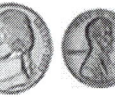

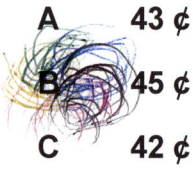

A   43 ¢

B   45 ¢

C   42 ¢

D   38 ¢

© Teachers' Treasures Publishing   Page 162

Name _____

PRACTICE

Common Core Standard 2.MD.C.8 – Measurement & Data

☐ **Diego has eight dimes, three nickels, and four pennies. How many cents does he have?**

A   99 ¢

B   89 ¢

C   98 ¢

D   88 ¢

Common Core Standard 2.MD.C.8 – Measurement & Data

☐ **JoAnn had 89 ¢. She spent five nickels on a binder. How much money does she have now?**

A   65 ¢   C   64 ¢

B   54 ¢   D   56 ¢

Common Core Standard 2.MD.C.8 – Measurement & Data

☐ **Look at the coins in the box. Which group of coins shows the same amount?**

Page 163

Name _____

PRACTICE

Common Core Standard 2.MD.C.8 – Measurement & Data

☐ Find the right number of coins.

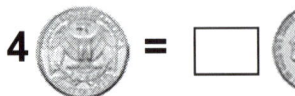

4 (quarter) = ☐ (nickel)

A   50

B   20

C   10

D   100

Common Core Standard 2.MD.C.8 – Measurement & Data

☐ How much are the coins below worth?

A   69 ¢

B   84 ¢

C   79 ¢

D   74 ¢

Common Core Standard 2.MD.C.8 – Measurement & Data

☐ Tyron spent six nickels on fruit snacks. Georgia spent four dimes on a bag of chips. How much did they spend in all?

A   70 ¢

B   80 ¢

C   65 ¢

D   75 ¢

© Teachers' Treasures Publishing

Name _____

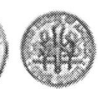

PRACTICE

Common Core Standard 2.MD.C.8 – Measurement & Data

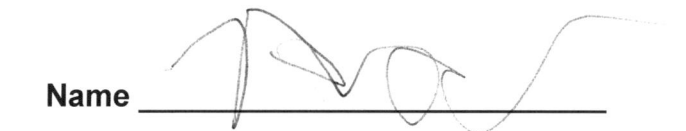

☐ **Armand buys a pack of juice boxes for 67¢. He pays the cashier with a one dollar bill. The cashier gives him his change back using the least amount of coins. Which coins does Armand receive?**

A (quarter, nickel, nickel, penny)

B (quarter, nickel, nickel, penny, penny, penny)

C (quarter, nickel, nickel, penny, penny, penny)

D (dime, dime, dime, penny, penny, penny)

Common Core Standard 2.MD.C.8 – Measurement & Data

☐ **Kevan had five quarters. He spent fifty cents on a toothbrush. How much money does he have now?**

A 65 ¢   C 70 ¢

B 75 ¢   D 60 ¢

Common Core Standard 2.MD.C.8 – Measurement & Data

☐ **Jordan has 2 quarters, 1 dime, and 2 nickels. How many cents does he have?**

A 80 ¢

B 78 ¢

C 70 ¢

D 85 ¢

© Teachers' Treasures Publishing   Page 165

Name _____

PRACTICE

Common Core Standard 2.MD.C.8 – Measurement & Data

☐ Which is not equal to 7 dimes?

A   one quarter, three dimes, three nickels

B   one quarter, two dimes, five nickels

C   two quarter, one dime, two nickels

D   two quarters, one dime, three nickels

Common Core Standard 2.MD.C.8 – Measurement & Data

☐ How much are the coins below worth?

A   97 ¢
B   87 ¢
C   88 ¢
D   79 ¢

75
+ 22

97

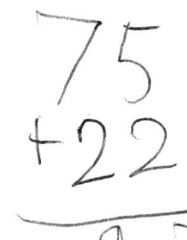

Common Core Standard 2.MD.C.8 – Measurement & Data

☐ How much is the money below worth?

A $1.40   C $1.50
B $1.45   D $1.85

25
+ 20

45

© Teachers' Treasures Publishing   Page 166

Name _____

ASSESSMENT

Common Core Standard 2.MD.C.8 – Measurement & Data

☐ Look at the coins in the box. Which group of coins shows the same amount?

A

B

C

D

Common Core Standard 2.MD.C.8 – Measurement & Data

☐ Find the right number of coins.

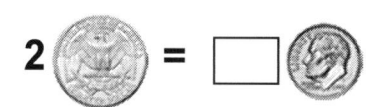

2 ⬤ = ☐ ⬤

A 4   C 10

B 5   D 6

Common Core Standard 2.MD.C.8 – Measurement & Data

☐ Hasmik had nine dimes. She spent thirty-five cents on a cupcake. How much money does she have now?

A   65 ¢   C   55 ¢

B   75 ¢   D   60 ¢

© Teachers' Treasures Publishing   Page 167

Name _____

ASSESSMENT

Common Core Standard 2.MD.C.8 – Measurement & Data

☐ Travis is saving to by a video game that costs $24. He had 80 quarters to start with. How much more money does he need to by the video game?

    A $4.00   C   40¢

    B   60 nickels   (D)   5 dimes

Common Core Standard 2.MD.C.8 – Measurement & Data

☐ Which is not equal to 9 nickels?

    A   one quarter, one dime, ten pennies

    B   one quarter, two dimes

    (C)   one quarter, two dimes, one nickel

    D   one quarters, one dime, two nickels

Common Core Standard 2.MD.C.8 – Measurement & Data

☐ Lee buys a box of her favorite cereal for 88¢. She pays the cashier with a one dollar bill. The cashier gives her change back using the least amount of coins. Which coins does Lee receive?

A   (quarter, nickel, nickel, penny)

(B)   (dime, nickel, penny, penny, penny)

C   (nickel, nickel, penny, penny)

D   (nickel, dime, penny, penny)

Name _____

DIAGNOSTIC

Common Core Standard 2.MD.D.9 – Measurement & Data

☐ A bakery sold cakes for four days in a row. Based on the data below choose which line plot is correct.

Days	Cakes sold
1	3
2	2
3	5
4	4

A
```
         X
         X  X
X        X  X
X  X     X  X
X  X     X  X
←--+--+--+--+--→
   1  2  3  4
   Number of days
```

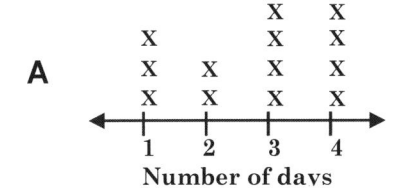

C 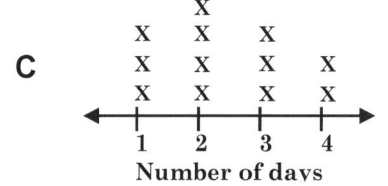
```
      X
X  X  X
X  X  X  X
X  X  X  X
←--+--+--+--+--→
   1  2  3  4
   Number of days
```

B (circled)
```
      X
      X
   X  X
   X  X
X  X  X  X
X  X  X  X
←--+--+--+--+--→
   1  2  3  4
   Number of days
```

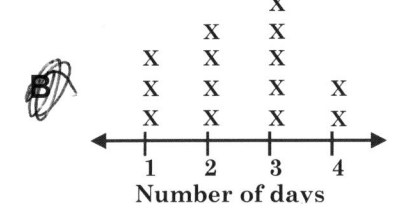

D
```
         X
         X
X        X
X  X  X  X
X  X  X  X
←--+--+--+--+--→
   1  2  3  4
   Number of days
```

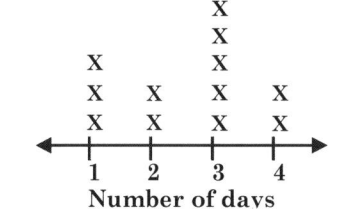

Common Core Standard 2.MD.D.9 – Measurement & Data

☐ A sports store sold bicycles for four days in a row. Choose the right line plot based on the data below.

Number of days	1	2	3	4
Number of bicycles	3	4	5	2

A (circled)
```
         X
      X  X
X  X  X  X
X  X  X  X
X  X  X  X
←--+--+--+--+--→
   1  2  3  4
   Number of days
```

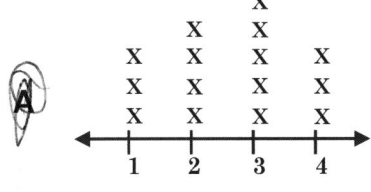

C
```
         X
      X  X X
X  X  X  X
X  X  X  X
X  X  X  X
←--+--+--+--+--→
   1  2  3  4
   Number of days
```

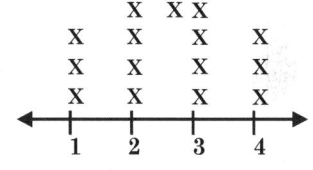

B
```
      X
      X
   X  X
   X  X  X
X  X  X  X
X  X  X  X
←--+--+--+--+--→
   1  2  3  4
   Number of days
```

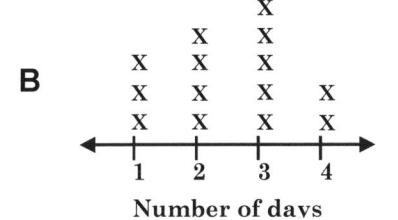

D
```
         X
         X
X  X  X
X  X  X  X
X  X  X  X
←--+--+--+--+--→
   1  2  3  4
   Number of days
```

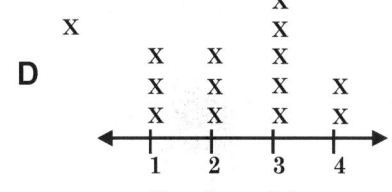

© Teachers' Treasures Publishing

Name _____

DIAGNOSTIC

Common Core Standard 2.MD.D.9 – Measurement & Data

☐ **Ms. Fitzhugh recorded the number of books her students read last semester. Look at the line plot she made and answer the questions below.**

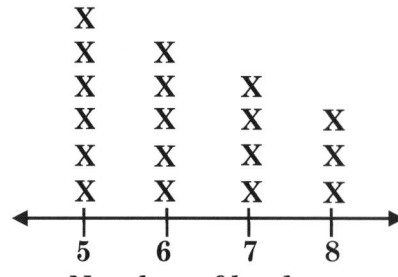

```
X
X   X
X   X   X
X   X   X   X
X   X   X   X
X   X   X   X
←─┼───┼───┼───┼─→
  5   6   7   8
   Number of books
```

How many students read 8 books?

A   6   C   4

B   5   D   3

Common Core Standard 2.MD.D.9 – Measurement & Data

☐ **A pizzeria sold mushroom pizzas four days in a row. Based on the data below choose which line plot is correct.**

Number of days	1	2	3	4
Number of mushroom pizzas	5	4	3	2

A
```
        X
    X   X
    X   X   X
    X   X   X   X
    X   X   X   X
←─┼───┼───┼───┼─→
  1   2   3   4
   Number of days
```

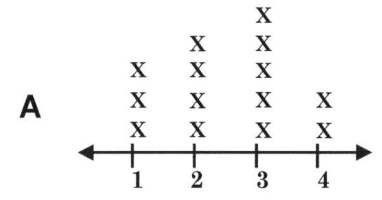

C
```
            X
            X
    X   X   X   X
    X   X   X   X
    X   X   X   X
←─┼───┼───┼───┼─→
  1   2   3   4
   Number of days
```

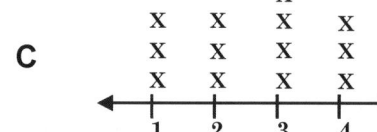

B
```
        X
        X
    X   X   X   X
    X   X   X   X
    X   X   X   X
←─┼───┼───┼───┼─→
  1   2   3   4
   Number of days
```

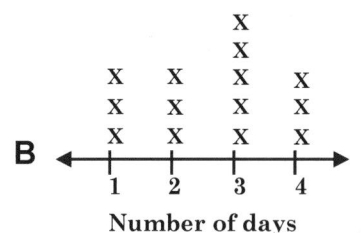

D
```
X
X
X   X
X   X   X
X   X   X   X
←─┼───┼───┼───┼─→
  1   2   3   4
   Number of days
```

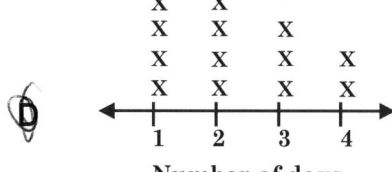

Name _____

PRACTICE

Common Core Standard 2.MD.D.9 – Measurement & Data

☐ A candy store sold giant gummy bears for three days straight. Choose the right line plot based on the data below.

Days	Giant gummy bears sold
1	4
2	6
3	2

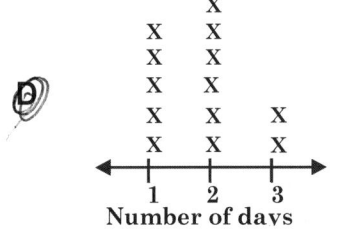

A

```
       X
    X  X
    X  X
    X  X  X
    X  X  X
    ─┼──┼──┼─→
     1  2  3
    Number of days
```

B

```
       X
    X  X
    X  X  X
    X  X  X
    X  X  X
    ─┼──┼──┼─→
     1  2  3
    Number of days
```

C

```
       X
       X
    X  X
    X  X
    X  X  X
    X  X  X
    ─┼──┼──┼─→
     1  2  3
    Number of days
```

(D)

```
       X
    X  X
    X  X
    X  X
    X  X  X
    X  X  X
    ─┼──┼──┼─→
     1  2  3
    Number of days
```

Common Core Standard 2.MD.D.9 – Measurement & Data

☐ A middle school choir is selling magazine subscriptions for a fundraiser. Using the line plot below answer the question.

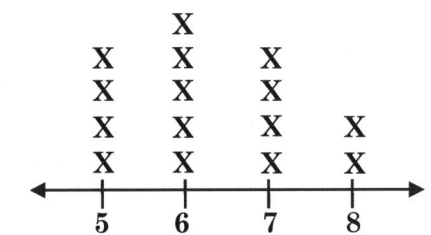

```
          X
    X  X  X
    X  X  X
    X  X  X  X
    X  X  X  X
    ─┼──┼──┼──┼─→
     5  6  7  8
    Number of magazine subscription
```

How many students sold 7 magazine subscriptions if each X = 2?

A   6   C   4

(B) 5   D   8

Name _____

PRACTICE

Common Core Standard 2.MD.D.9 – Measurement & Data

☐ Coach recorded the number of soccer players who showed up on practice days. Based on the data in tally chart choose the correct line plot.

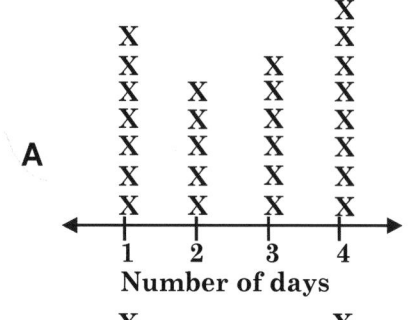

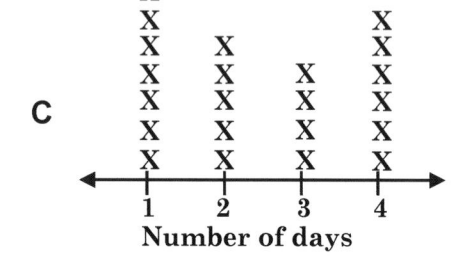

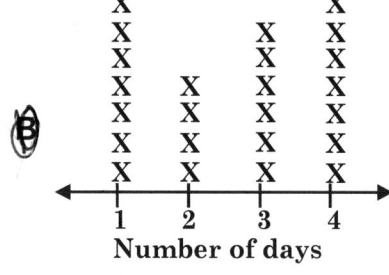

Practice Days	Number of players
1	ⵘⵘ ‖
2	ⵘⵘ
3	ⵘⵘ ‖
4	ⵘⵘ ‖‖‖

A, B (circled), C, D — line plots of Number of days 1–4.

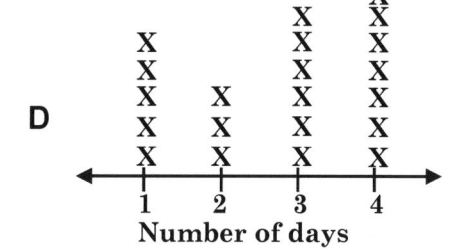

Common Core Standard 2.MD.D.9 – Measurement & Data

☐ A movie theater tracked the number of tickets sold for a new movie during the first four days. How many tickets did the theater sell on the second day if each X = 100?

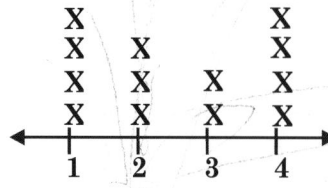

A   200   C   400

B (circled) 500   D   300

© Teachers' Treasures Publishing   Page 172

Name _____

PRACTICE

Common Core Standard 2.MD.D.9 – Measurement & Data

☐ **Natasha counted the number of matches won by her favorite tennis players during the Wimbledon Championships. Based on the data in tally chart below choose the correct line plot.**

Number of tennis matches won	Number of tennis players
0	6
1	4
2	7
3	5
4	3

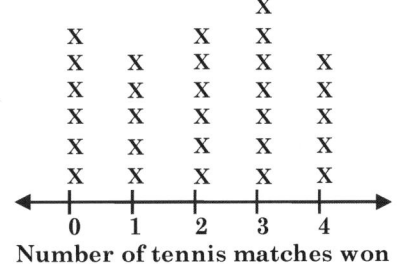

A
```
        X
X       X
X       X   X
X   X   X   X
X   X   X   X   X
X   X   X   X   X
X   X   X   X   X
←—+—+—+—+—+—→
  0   1   2   3   4
Number of tennis matches won
```

C
```
X       X
X       X   X
X   X   X   X   X
X   X   X   X   X
X   X   X   X   X
X   X   X   X   X
←—+—+—+—+—+—→
  0   1   2   3   4
Number of tennis matches won
```

B
```
            X
X       X   X
X   X   X   X   X
X   X   X   X   X
X   X   X   X   X
X   X   X   X   X
X   X   X   X   X
←—+—+—+—+—+—→
  0   1   2   3   4
Number of tennis matches won
```

D
```
            X
        X   X
X       X   X
X   X   X   X   X
X   X   X   X   X
X   X   X   X   X
X   X   X   X   X
←—+—+—+—+—+—→
  0   1   2   3   4
Number of tennis matches won
```

Common Core Standard 2.MD.D.9 – Measurement & Data

☐ **A pet store tracked the number of puppies sold during the last five days. On which day did the pet store sell the least puppies?**

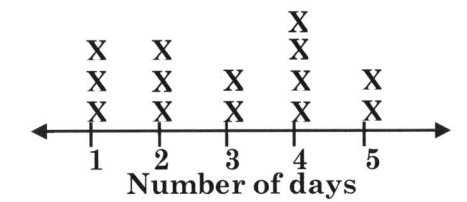

```
                X
    X       X   X
    X   X   X   X
    X   X   X   X   X
    X   X   X   X   X
←—+—+—+—+—+—→
  1   2   3   4   5
Number of days
```

A   days 2 and 4   C   days 3 and 4

B   days 2 and 3   D   days 3 and 5

© Teachers' Treasures Publishing   Page 173

Name _____

PRACTICE

Common Core Standard 2.MD.D.9 – Measurement & Data

☐ A snow cone stand sold orange-mango flavored snow cones for 4 days straight. Based on the data in tally chart below choose the correct line plot.

Number of sales	Number of orange-mango snow cones
1									
2								
3						
4								

A

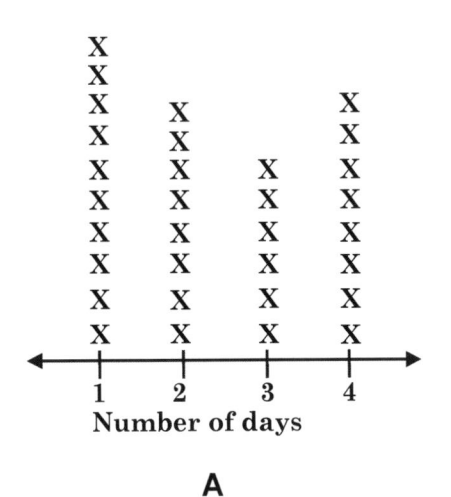

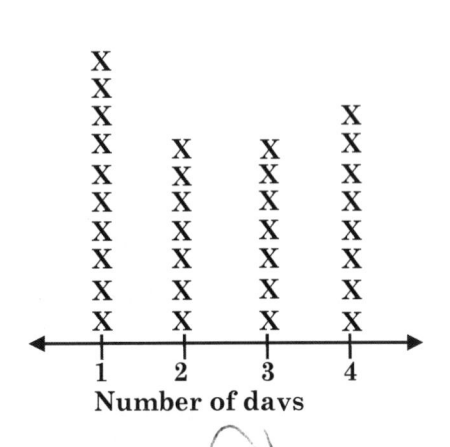

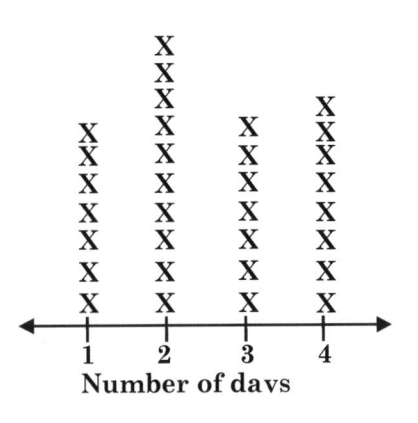

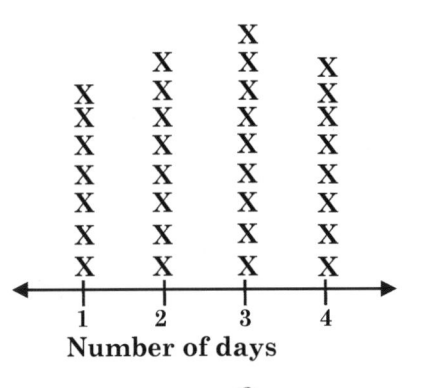

B

C

D

Name _____

ASSESSMENT

Common Core Standard 2.MD.D.9 – Measurement & Data

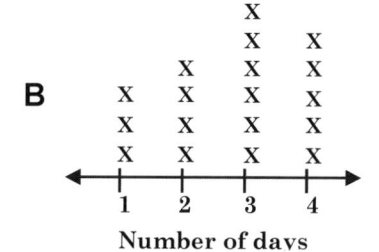

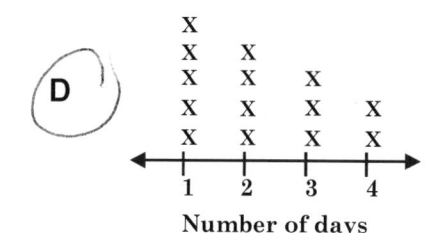

☐ **Kindergarteners were asked for their favorite number. Using the line plot below answer the question.**

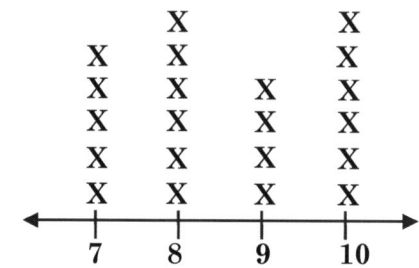

```
                X       X
        X       X       X
        X       X       X
        X       X   X   X
        X       X   X   X
        X       X   X   X
        X       X   X   X
    ←———+———+———+———+———→
        7       8   9   10
      Kindergarteners' favorite numbers
```

How many kindergarteners have a favorite number that is less than 9?

A   6   C   11

(B)   5   D   10

Common Core Standard 2.MD.D.9 – Measurement & Data

☐ **A swimming instructor kept track of the laps each kid swam. Based on the data below choose which line plot is correct.**

Number of laps	1	2	3	4
Number of kids	3	4	6	5

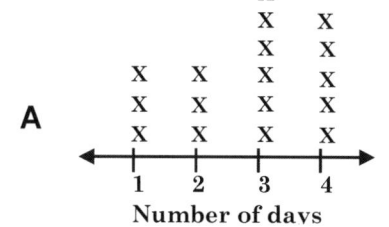

A – line plot with 1:4, 2:4, 3:6, 4:5
B – line plot with 1:3, 2:4, 3:6, 4:4
C – line plot with 1:4, 2:4, 3:5, 4:4
(D) – line plot with 1:3, 2:4, 3:6, 4:5

© Teachers' Treasures Publishing   Page 175

Name _____

ASSESSMENT

Common Core Standard 2.MD.D.9 – Measurement & Data

☐ Principal Lange bought bagels for her Teachers five days in a row. Using the line plot below answer the question.

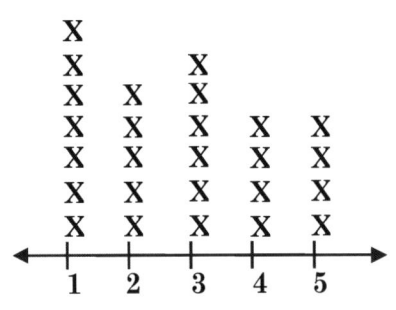

```
X
X       X
X   X   X
X   X   X   X   X
X   X   X   X   X
X   X   X   X   X
X   X   X   X   X
←—+—+—+—+—+—→
  1   2   3   4   5
    Number of days
```

How many bagels did she buy during the first two days?

A   7   C   11

B   12   (D) 10

Common Core Standard 2.MD.D.9 – Measurement & Data

☐ Noah's woodshop was building dog houses. Look at the data below and choose the correct matching line plot.

Weeks	Dog Houses Built
1	4
2	5
3	3

A
```
    X
X   X
X   X
X   X   X
X   X   X
←+—+—+→
 1  2  3
Number of weeks
```

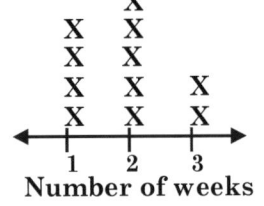

(C)
```
    X
    X
X   X
X   X
X   X   X
X   X   X
←+—+—+→
 1  2  3
Number of weeks
```

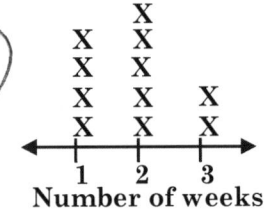

B
```
    X
X   X
X   X   X
X   X   X
X   X   X
←+—+—+→
 1  2  3
Number of weeks
```

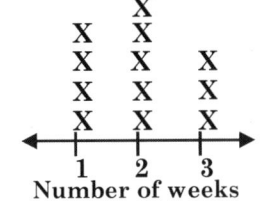

D
```
    X
X   X
X   X
X   X
X   X   X
X   X   X
←+—+—+→
 1  2  3
Number of weeks
```

© Teachers' Treasures Publishing

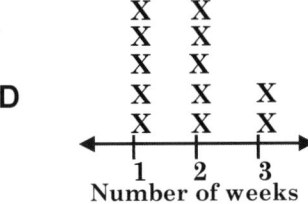

Name _____

DIAGNOSTIC

Common Core Standard 2.MD.D.10 – Measurement & Data

Second graders voted on their favorite type of pet. Which graph below best represents the data?

Pet	Dog	Cat	Rabbit	Parrot
Number of pets	7	4	3	5

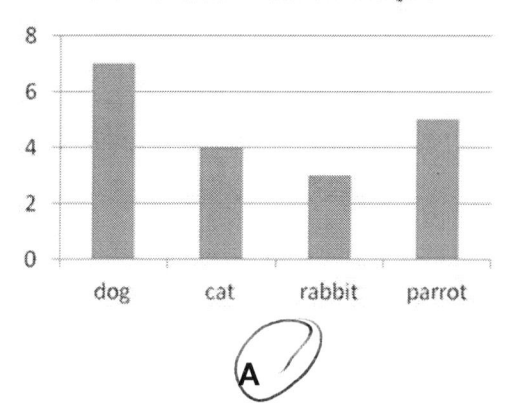

A (circled)

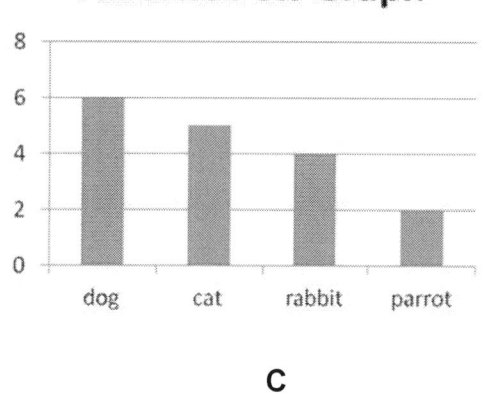

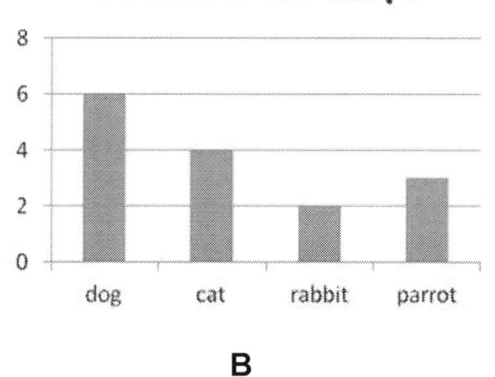

B

C

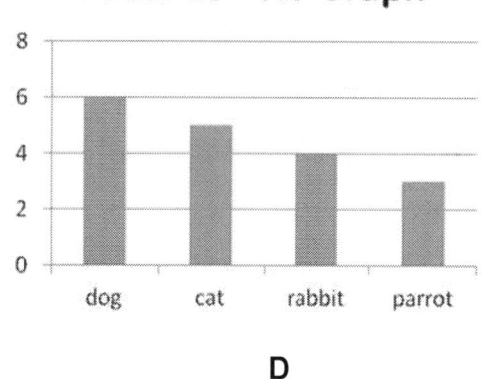

D

Common Core Standard MD.D.10 – Measurement & Data

Based on the graph above which pet is the least favorite among the second graders?

A   dog

B   cat

C   rabbit

D   parrot (circled)

© Teachers' Treasures Publishing

Name _____

DIAGNOSTIC

Common Core Standard MD.D.10 – Measurement & Data

☐ Look at the pictograph below. How many cans did Liam recycle?

Recycling drive	
Liam	🥫🥫🥫🥫
Henry	🥫🥫🥫🥫🥫
Hayk	🥫🥫🥫🥫🥫🥫

A   5   C   4

B   7   D   6

Common Core Standard MD.D.10 – Measurement & Data

☐ Irene's class voted on their favorite Winter Olympics games. Which game was the most popular among Irene's classmates?

Favorite Winter Olimpics Sports

A   Hockey   C   Curling

B   Figure Skating   D   Bobsled

© Teachers' Treasures Publishing

Name _____

PRACTICE

Common Core Standard MD.D.10 – Measurement & Data

☐ **Girls voted on their favorite shoes. How many girls chose boots as their favorite?**

Shoe Votes	
Boots	👢👢👢👢👢👢
Sneakers	👟👟👟👟
Flip Flops	👡👡👡👡👡👡👡👡

(A) 5   C   4

B   6   D   8

Common Core Standard MD.D.10 – Measurement & Data

☐ **Based on the graph above how many more girls like flip flops than sneakers?**

A   4   C   6

B   5   (D)   3

Common Core Standard MD.D.10 – Measurement & Data

☐ **Based on the graph above how many more girls prefer boots to sneakers?**

A   3   C   1

(B)   4   D   2

© Teachers' Treasures Publishing   Page 179

Name _____

PRACTICE

Common Core Standard MD.D.10 – Measurement & Data

☐ Students were asked what their favorite subject was. Which graph below best represent the data?

Subjects	Math	Art	History
Number of students	9	6	4

A — Student's Favorite Subjects (Math 8, Art 5, History 4)

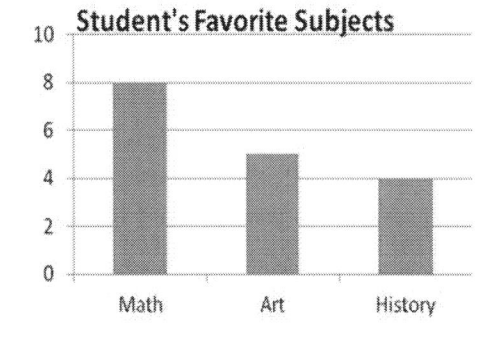

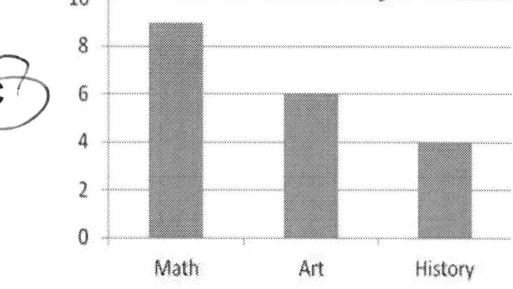

B — Student's Favorite Subjects (Math 4, Art 6, History 9)

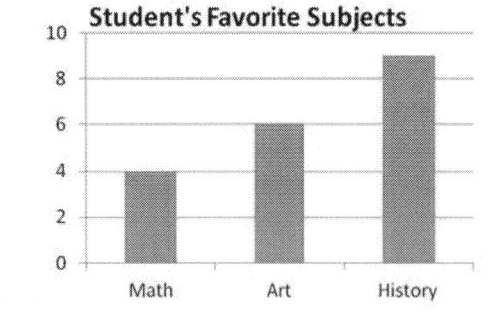

C (circled) — Student's Favorite Subjects (Math 9, Art 6, History 4)

D — Student's Favorite Subjects (Math 7, Art 5, History 6)

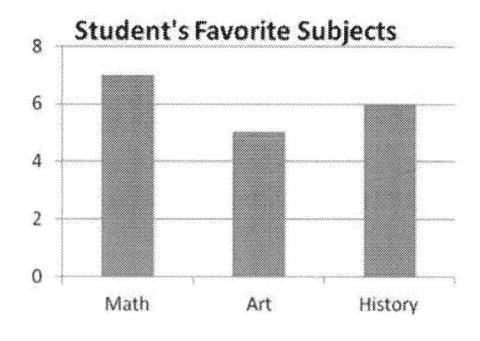

Common Core Standard MD.D.10 – Measurement & Data

☐ Based on the data above how many students like math and history?

A   12
B   5
C   13
D (circled) 10

Name _____

PRACTICE

Common Core Standard MD.D.10 – Measurement & Data

☐ **Kids went shopping for new clothes. Look at the pictograph below and answer the following questions.**

Purchased T-Shirts	
Kathryn	👕 👕 👕 👕 1
Michael	👕 👕 👕
Steve	👕 👕 👕 👕 👕
Samantha	👕 👕 1
Andrew	👕 👕 👕 1

Each 👕 = 2 T-shirts   Each 1 = 1 T-shirt

How many T-shirts did Samantha buy?

A   5   C   2

B   6   D   3

Common Core Standard MD.D10 – Measurement & Data

☐ **How many T-shirts did Michael and Andrew buy together?**

A   12   C   10

B   7   D   13

© Teachers' Treasures Publishing

Name _____

PRACTICE

Common Core Standard MD.D.10 – Measurement & Data

☐ A pizzeria monitored the number of pizzas sold last month. Look at the bar graph below and answer the questions.

Number Of Pizzas Sold

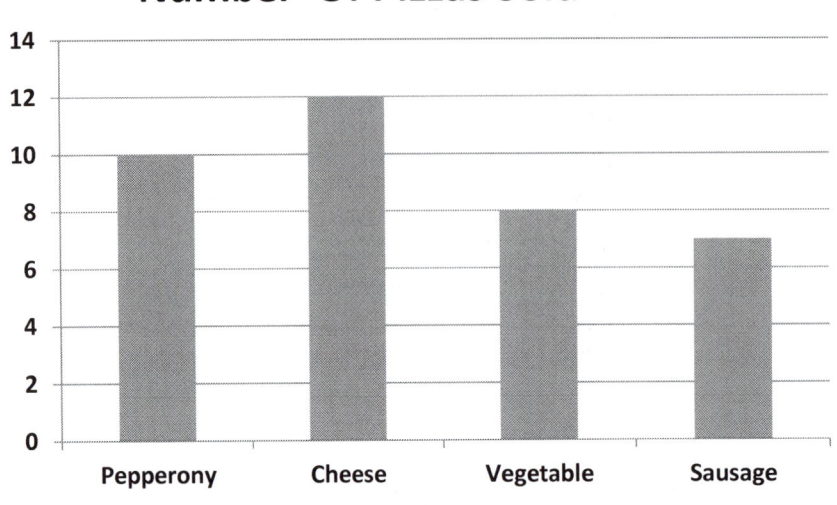

(Bar graph: Pepperony = 10, Cheese = 12, Vegetable = 8, Sausage = 7)

How many more cheese pizzas were sold than sausage?

A   4   C   7

(B)   5   D   12

Common Core Standard MD.D.10 – Measurement & Data

☐ How many pizzas did the pizzeria sell altogether?

(A)   37   C   26

B   36   D   34

© Teachers' Treasures Publishing

Name _____

ASSESSMENT

Common Core Standard MD.D.10 – Measurement & Data

☐ A charity collected used clothes for hurricane survivors. Looking at the bar graph below answer the following question.

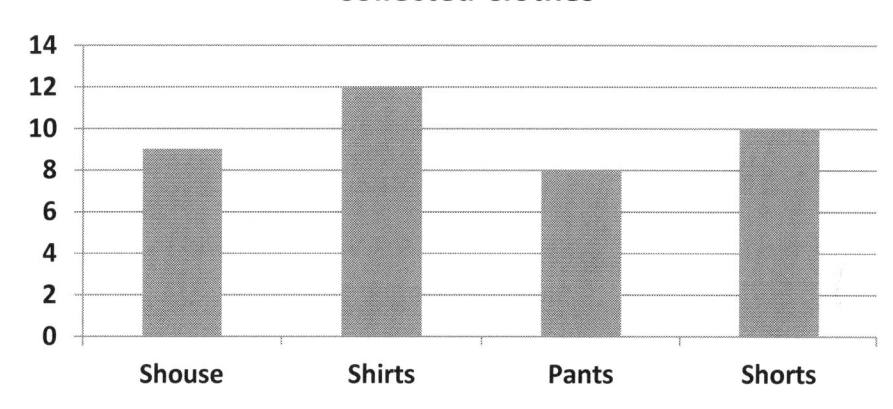

Collected Clothes

How many pieces of clothing did the charity collect?

A   38   C   39

B   28   D   29

Common Core Standard MD.D.10 – Measurement & Data

☐ Armen was cleaning up his toy chest. He made a pictograph of his toys. How many more robots does he have than airplanes?

Armen's Toys	
Airplanes	✈ ✈ ✈ ✈ ✈
Trucks	🚒 🚒 🚒 🚒
Robots	🤖 🤖 🤖 🤖 🤖 🤖 🤖

A   4   C   3

B   2   D   5

© Teachers' Treasures Publishing

Name _____

ASSESSMENT

Common Core Standard MD.D.10 – Measurement & Data

☐ The store recorded the number of books sold last week. Which bar graph matches the data below?

Books	Fiction	Comic	Mystery	Biography
Number of books	5	8	6	2

A

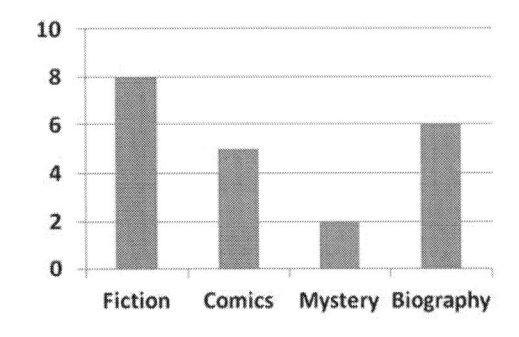

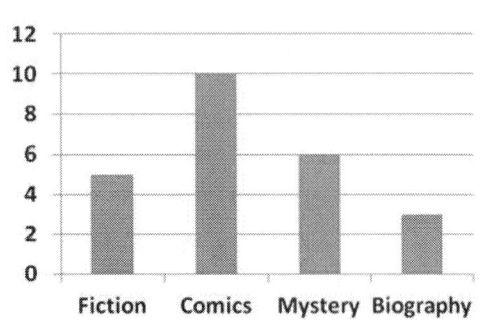

B

C

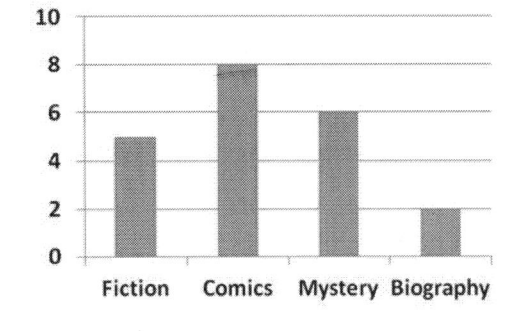

D

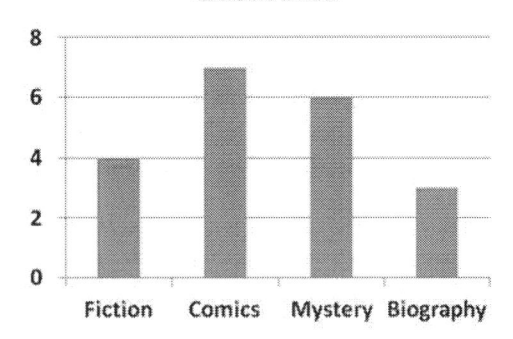

Common Core Standard MD.D.10 – Measurement & Data

☐ Based on the data above, how many more comics were sold than mystery books last week?

A   2

B   1

C   3

D   4

© Teachers' Treasures Publishing

Page 184

Name _____

DIAGNOSTIC

Common Core Standard 2.G.A.1 – Geometry

☐ **What is the name of the figure below?**

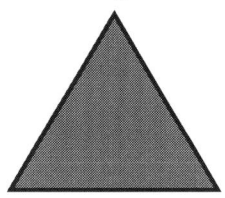

A   Square

B   Hexagon

C   Oval

D   Triangle

Common Core Standard 2.G.A.1 – Geometry

☐ **How many sides does the parallelogram below have?**

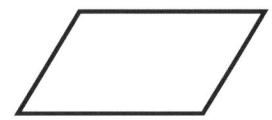

A   3   C   2

B   4   D   5

Common Core Standard 2.G.A.1 – Geometry

☐ **How many edges does the figure below have?**

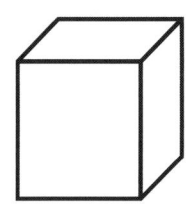

A   8   C   12

B   10   D   16

© Teachers' Treasures Publishing

Name _____

DIAGNOSTIC

Common Core Standard 2.G.A.1 – Geometry

☐ What is the name of the figure below?

A	Oval	C	Quadrilateral
B	Circle	D	Cube

Common Core Standard 2.G.A.1 – Geometry

☐ How many vertices does the figure below have?

A	8	C	5
B	4	D	6

Common Core Standard 2.G.A.1 – Geometry

☐ What is the name of the figure below?

A	Cone	C	Cube
B	Cylinder	D	Oval

© Teachers' Treasures Publishing

Name _____

PRACTICE

Common Core Standard 2.G.A.1 – Geometry

☐ **What figure is this?**

A   Hexagon   C   Nonagon

B   Octagon   D   Pentagon

Common Core Standard 2.G.A.1 – Geometry

☐ **How many sides does this figure have?**

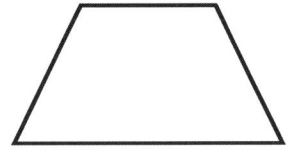

A   4   C   5

B   6   D   8

Common Core Standard 2.G.A.1 – Geometry

☐ **What is the name of the figure below?**

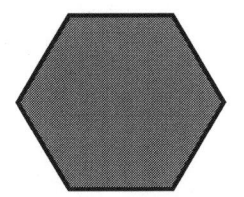

A   Pentagon   C   Quadrilateral

B   Parallelogram   D   Hexagon

© Teachers' Treasures Publishing

Name _____

PRACTICE

Common Core Standard 2.G.A.1 – Geometry

☐ **What figure is this?**

A   Oval   C   Square

B   Parallelogram   D   Triangle

Common Core Standard 2.G.A.1 – Geometry

☐ **What is the name of the figure below?**

A   Cube   C   Square

B   Pentagon   D   Oval

Common Core Standard 2.G.A.1 – Geometry

☐ **What figure is this?**

A   Parallelogram   C   Square

B   Diamond   D   Trapezoid

© Teachers' Treasures Publishing

Name _____

PRACTICE

Common Core Standard 2.G.A.1 – Geometry

☐ Which shape has the most sides?

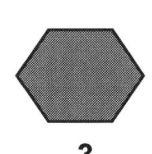

1 2 3 4

A   1
B   4
C   2
D   3

Common Core Standard 2.G.A.1 – Geometry

☐ What is the name of the figure below?

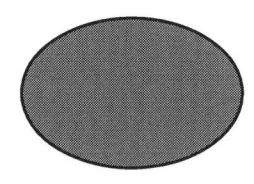

A   Square
B   Oval
C   Cylinder
D   Hexagon

Common Core Standard 2.G.A.1 – Geometry

☐ What figure is this?

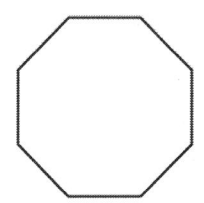

A   Hexagon
B   Octagon
C   Pentagon
D   Parallelogram

© Teachers' Treasures Publishing

Name _____

PRACTICE

Common Core Standard 2.G.A.1 – Geometry

☐ What is the name of the figure below?

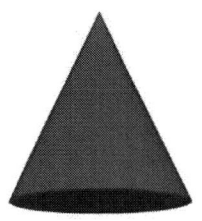

A	Triangle	C	Trapezoid
B	Cone	D	Cube

Common Core Standard 2.G.A.1 – Geometry

☐ How many sets of parallel sides does the figure below has?

A	2	C	4
B	3	D	6

Common Core Standard 2.G.A.1 – Geometry

☐ What figure is this?

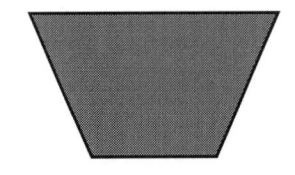

A	Parallelogram	C	Square
B	Cube	D	Trapezoid

© Teachers' Treasures Publishing

Page 190

Name _____

ASSESSMENT

Common Core Standard 2.G.A.1 – Geometry

☐   How many vertices does this figure have?

A	8	C	6
B	4	D	10

Common Core Standard 2.G.A.1 – Geometry

☐   How many sets of parallel sides does the parallelogram have?

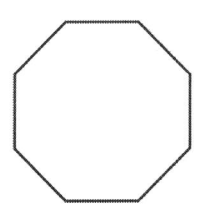

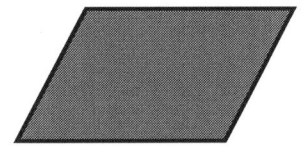

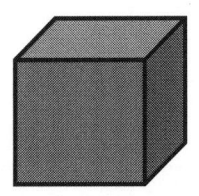

A	4	C	2
B	1	D	none

Common Core Standard 2.G.A.1 – Geometry

☐   How many vertices does this figure have?

A	9	C	6
B	8	D	12

© Teachers' Treasures Publishing

Page 191

Name _____

ASSESSMENT

Common Core Standard 2.G.A.1 – Geometry

☐ How many sides does this figure have?

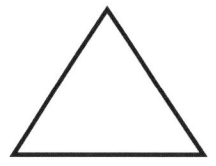

A   4   C   3

B   2   D   6

Common Core Standard 2.G.A.1 – Geometry

☐ What figure has 4 equal sides and all the angle are right angles?

A   Trapezoid

B   Triangle

C   Diamond

D   Square

Common Core Standard 2.G.A.1 – Geometry

☐ How many vertices does the figure below have?

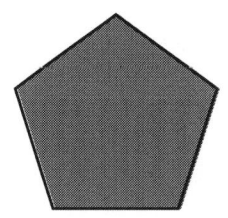

A   6   C   4

B   5   D   3

© Teachers' Treasures Publishing

Name _____

DIAGNOSTIC

Common Core Standard 2.G.A.2 – Geometry

☐ **Count the squares inside the rectangle. How many squares is the rectangle made of?**

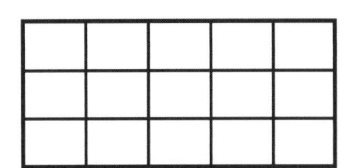

A   15   C   14

B   10   D   16

Common Core Standard 2.G.A.2 – Geometry

☐ **This shape is made out of unit squares. How many unit squares are there?**

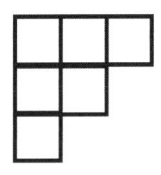

A   6   C   5

B   7   D   8

Common Core Standard 2.G.A.2 – Geometry

☐ **Count the squares inside the rectangle. How many squares is the rectangle made of?**

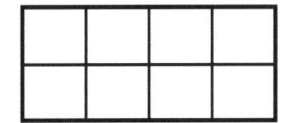

A   10   C   6

B   12   D   8

© Teachers' Treasures Publishing

Name _____

DIAGNOSTIC

Common Core Standard 2.G.A.2 – Geometry

☐ This shape is made out of unit squares. How many unit squares are there?

A   10   C   9
B   8   D   11

Common Core Standard 2.G.A.2 – Geometry

☐ Count the squares inside the rectangle. How many squares is the rectangle made of?

A   10   C   14
B   12   D   9

Common Core Standard 2.G.A.2 – Geometry

☐ This shape is made out of unit squares. What is the area of the figure?

A   14 square units   C   15 square units
B   13 square units   D   12 square units

© Teachers' Treasures Publishing

Page 194

Name _____

PRACTICE

Common Core Standard 2.G.A.2 – Geometry

☐ **This shape is made out of unit squares. How many unit squares are there?**

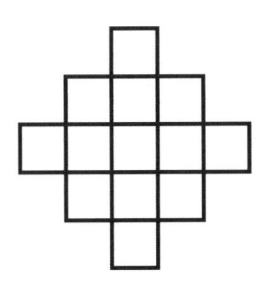

A   13   C   12

B   14   D   11

Common Core Standard 2.G.A.2 – Geometry

☐ **Divide the rectangle into 1 row and 9 columns. Count the squares inside the rectangle. How many are there?**

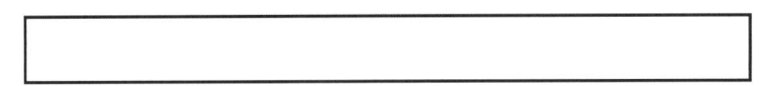

A   8   C   7

B   9   D   10

Common Core Standard 2.G.A.2 – Geometry

☐ **This shape is made out of unit squares. What is the area of the figure?**

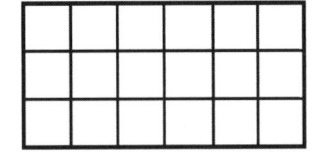

A   12 square units   C   24 square units

B   16 square units   D   18 square units

© Teachers' Treasures Publishing

Name _____

PRACTICE

Common Core Standard 2.G.A.2 – Geometry

☐ This shape is made out of unit squares. What is the area of the figure?

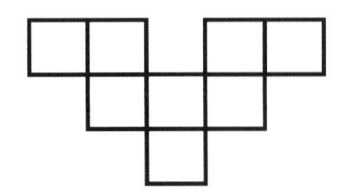

| A | 7 square units | C | 8 square units |
| B | 10 square units | D | 9 square units |

Common Core Standard 2.G.A.2 – Geometry

☐ Divide the rectangle into 2 rows and 3 columns. Count the squares inside the rectangle. How many are there?

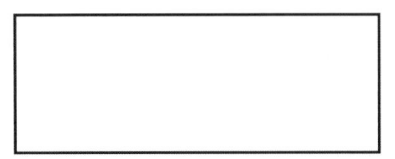

| A | 8 | C | 7 |
| B | 9 | D | 6 |

Common Core Standard 2.G.A.2 – Geometry

☐ This shape is made out of unit squares. How many unit squares are there?

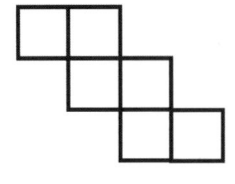

| A | 10 | C | 8 |
| B | 6 | D | 7 |

© Teachers' Treasures Publishing   Page 196

Name _____

PRACTICE

Common Core Standard 2.G.A.2 – Geometry

☐ **Count the squares inside the rectangle. How many squares is the rectangle made of?**

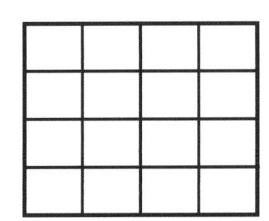

A	10	C	14
B	12	D	16

Common Core Standard 2.G.A.2 – Geometry

☐ **This shape is made out of unit squares. What is the area of the figure?**

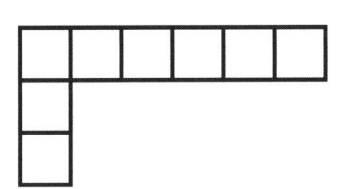

A	10 square units	C	9 square units
B	7 square units	D	8 square units

Common Core Standard 2.G.A.2 – Geometry

☐ **Divide the rectangle into 2 rows and 5 columns. Count the squares inside the rectangle. How many are there?**

A	12	C	8
B	10	D	6

© Teachers' Treasures Publishing

Name _____

PRACTICE

Common Core Standard 2.G.A.2 – Geometry

☐ This shape is made out of unit squares. What is the area of the figure?

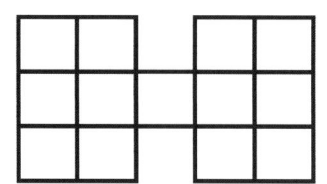

A   7 square units   C   13 square units

B   12 square units   D   9 square units

Common Core Standard 2.G.A.2 – Geometry

☐ Count the squares inside the rectangle. How many squares is the rectangle made of?

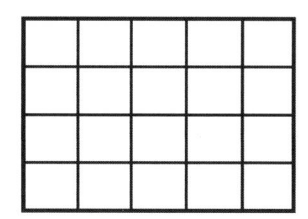

A   10   C   15

B   18   D   20

Common Core Standard 2.G.A.2 – Geometry

☐ This shape is made out of unit squares. How many unit squares are there?

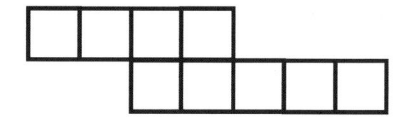

A   10   C   8

B   9   D   7

© Teachers' Treasures Publishing

Name _____

ASSESSMENT

Common Core Standard 2.G.A.2 – Geometry

☐ This shape is made out of unit squares. What is the area of the figure?

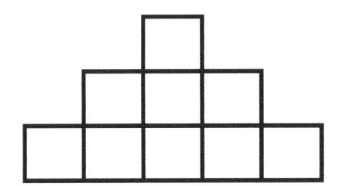

A   7 square units   C   8 square units

B   10 square units   D   9 square units

Common Core Standard 2.G.A.2 – Geometry

☐ Divide the rectangle into 3 rows and 4 columns. Count the squares inside the rectangle. How many are there?

A   12   C   8

B   10   D   6

Common Core Standard 2.G.A.2 – Geometry

☐ This shape is made out of unit squares. How many unit squares are there?

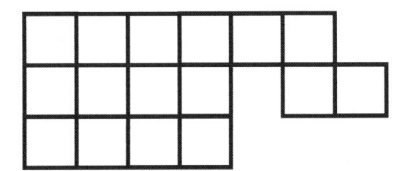

A   15   C   16

B   18   D   17

© Teachers' Treasures Publishing

Name _____

ASSESSMENT

Common Core Standard 2.G.A.2 – Geometry

☐ A rectangle has 4 rows and 5 columns. How many squares are in the rectangle?

A   20   C   15

B   25   D   10

Common Core Standard 2.G.A.2 – Geometry

☐ Count the squares inside the rectangle. How many squares is the rectangle made of?

A   7   C   6

B   9   D   8

Common Core Standard 2.G.A.2 – Geometry

☐ This shape is made out of unit squares. What is the area of the figure?

A   10 square units   C   13 square units

B   12 square units   D   9 square units

© Teachers' Treasures Publishing

Name _____

DIAGNOSTIC

Common Core Standard 2.G.A.3 – Geometry

☐ Which shape is divided into equal parts?

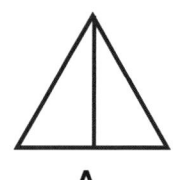

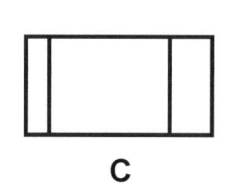

A   B   C   D

A   B   C   C
B   A   D   D

Common Core Standard 2.G.A.3 – Geometry

☐ What part of the figure is shaded?

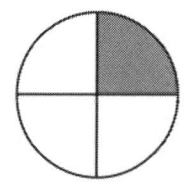

A $\dfrac{1}{4}$ C $\dfrac{2}{5}$

B $\dfrac{2}{3}$ D $\dfrac{3}{3}$

Common Core Standard 2.G.A.3 – Geometry

☐ Which figure shows fourths?

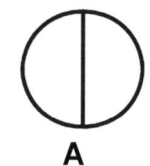

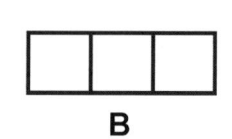

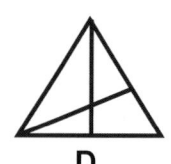

A   B   C   D

A   A   C   B
B   C   D   D

© Teachers' Treasures Publishing

Name _____

DIAGNOSTIC

Common Core Standard 2.G.A.3 – Geometry

☐ **What part of the figure is shaded?**

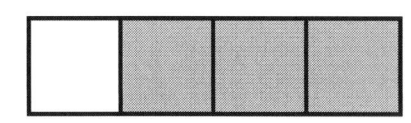

A $\frac{3}{4}$ C $\frac{2}{3}$

B $\frac{1}{4}$ D $\frac{1}{3}$

Common Core Standard 2.G.A.3 – Geometry

☐ **Which shape is divided into equal parts?**

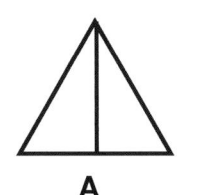

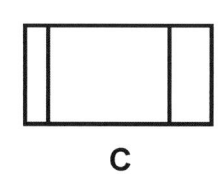

A   B   C   D

A   D   C   B
B   A   D   C

Common Core 2.G.A.3 – Geometry

☐ **Which shape shows the fraction $\frac{3}{5}$?**

A   C

B   D

© Teachers' Treasures Publishing   Page 202

Name _____

PRACTICE

Common Core Standard 2.G.A.3 – Geometry

☐ **Which figure shows halves?**

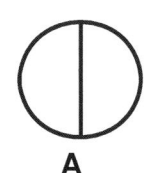

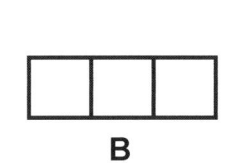

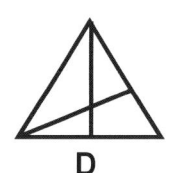

A   B   C   D

A   A   C   B

B   C   D   D

Common Core Standard 2.G.A.3 – Geometry

☐ **What part of the figure is shaded?**

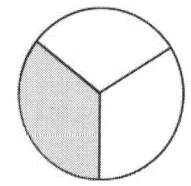

A $\dfrac{1}{4}$ C $\dfrac{2}{5}$

B $\dfrac{2}{3}$ D $\dfrac{1}{3}$

Common Core Standard 2.G.A.3 – Geometry

☐ **Choose the fraction for the whole shown below.**

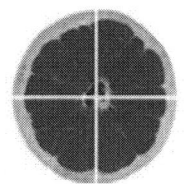

A $\dfrac{4}{4}$ C $\dfrac{4}{5}$

B $\dfrac{2}{3}$ D $\dfrac{1}{3}$

© Teachers' Treasures Publishing

Name _____

PRACTICE

Common Core Standard 2.G.A.3 – Geometry

☐ **Which shape is divided into equal parts?**

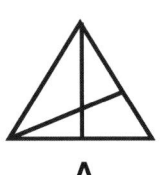

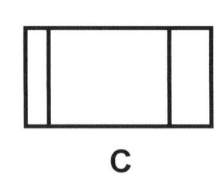

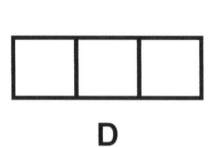

A   B   C   C

B   A   D   D

Common Core Standard 2.G.A.3 – Geometry

☐ **What part of the figure is shaded?**

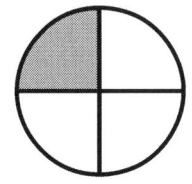

A $\frac{1}{4}$ C $\frac{2}{5}$

B $\frac{2}{3}$ D $\frac{1}{3}$

Common Core Standard 2.G.A.3 – Geometry

☐ **Which shape shows the fraction $\frac{1}{3}$?**

A   C

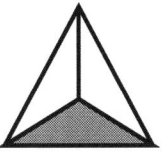

B   D

© Teachers' Treasures Publishing

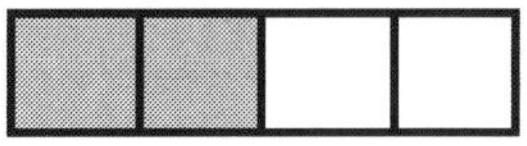

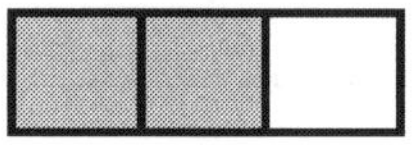

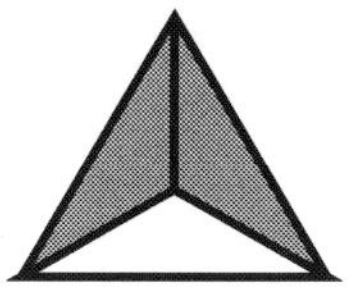

Name _____

PRACTICE

Common Core Standard 2.G.A.3 – Geometry

☐ **Choose the fraction for the whole shown below.**

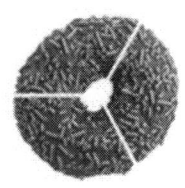

A $\dfrac{4}{4}$

B $\dfrac{2}{3}$

C $\dfrac{4}{5}$

D $\dfrac{3}{3}$

Common Core Standard 2.G.A.3 – Geometry

☐ **What part of the figure is shaded?**

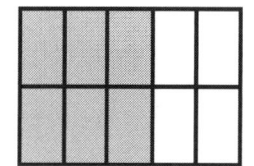

A $\dfrac{6}{8}$

B $\dfrac{4}{10}$

C $\dfrac{6}{10}$

D $\dfrac{4}{6}$

Common Core Standard 2.G.A.3 – Geometry

☐ **Which figure shows fourths?**

A   B   C   D

A A

B C

C B

D D

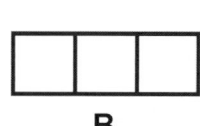

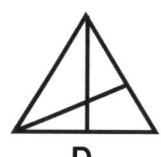

© Teachers' Treasures Publishing

Name _____

PRACTICE

Common Core Standard 2.G.A.3 – Geometry

☐ Which shape shows the fraction $\frac{4}{6}$?

A   C

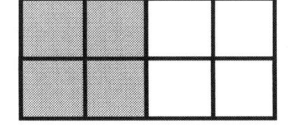

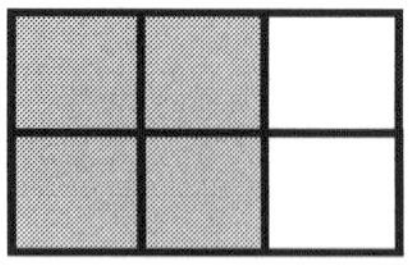

B 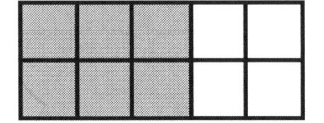   D

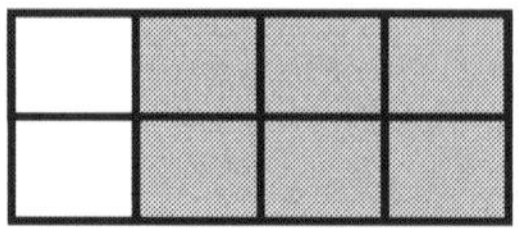

Common Core Standard 2.G.A.3 – Geometry

☐ What part of the figure is shaded?

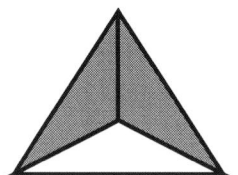

A $\frac{1}{4}$ C $\frac{2}{5}$

B $\frac{2}{3}$ D $\frac{1}{3}$

Common Core Standard 2.G.A.3 – Geometry

☐ Which shapes are divided into equal parts?

A   B   C   D

A   A and B   C   B and C

B   A and D   D   D and B

© Teachers' Treasures Publishing

Page 206

Name _____

ASSESSMENT

Common Core Standard 2.G.A.3 – Geometry

☐ Which figure shows halves?

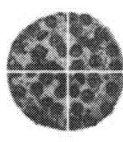

A   B   C   D

A   A   C   B

B   C   D   D

Common Core Standard 2.G.A.3 – Geometry

☐ What part of the figure is shaded?

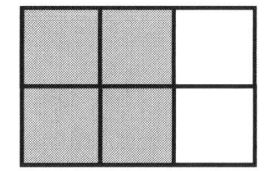

A $\frac{6}{8}$ C $\frac{4}{8}$

B $\frac{4}{6}$ D $\frac{4}{4}$

Common Core Standard 2.G.A.3 – Geometry

☐ Which shape shows the fraction $\frac{6}{10}$?

A 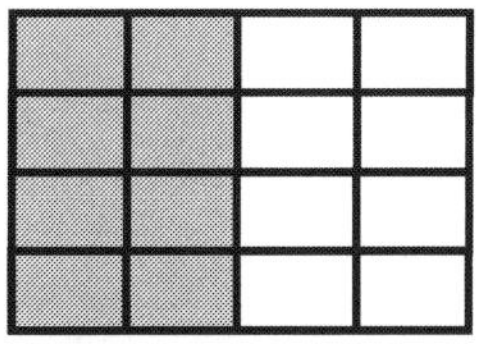   C

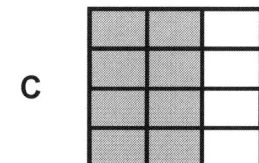

B 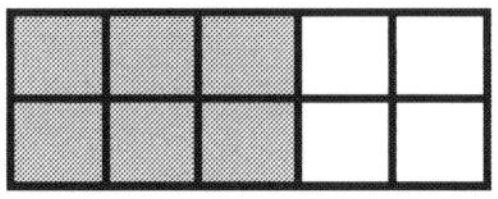   D

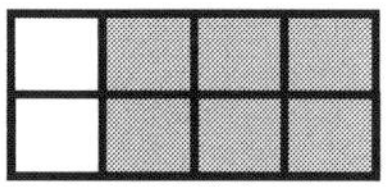

© Teachers' Treasures Publishing

Name _____

ASSESSMENT

Common Core Standard 2.G.A.3 – Geometry

☐ **Choose the fraction for the whole shown below.**

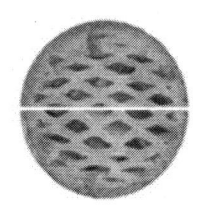

A $\dfrac{2}{4}$ C $\dfrac{4}{5}$

B $\dfrac{2}{2}$ D $\dfrac{1}{3}$

Common Core Standard 2.G.A.3 – Geometry

☐ **Which figures show thirds?**

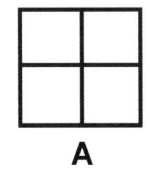

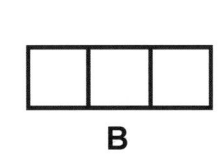

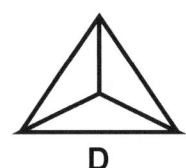

A   B   C   D

A   A and D   C   B and D

B   B and C   D   A and C

Common Core Standard 2.G.A.3 – Geometry

☐ **What part of the figure is shaded?**

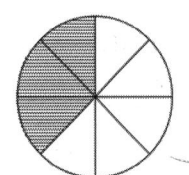

A $\dfrac{6}{8}$ C $\dfrac{4}{8}$

B $\dfrac{3}{8}$ D $\dfrac{3}{4}$

© Teachers' Treasures Publishing

ANSWER KEY

2.OA.A.1 ✓

Page 1 .... B, B, C
Page 2 .... C, C, D
Page 3 .... B, C, A
Page 4 .... D, B, D
Page 5 .... C, C, A
Page 6 .... D, B, B
Page 7 .... A, C, A
Page 8 .... A, D, C

2.OA.B.2

Page 9 .... B, C, D
Page 10 .... A, D, C
Page 11 .... A, B, C
Page 12 .... A, C, D
Page 13 .... D, A, B
Page 14 .... D, A, B
Page 15 .... C, C, A
Page 16 .... C, B, B

2.OA.C.3

Page 17 .... A, C, B
Page 18 .... C, C, A
Page 19 .... C, C, A
Page 20 .... B, A, B
Page 21 .... C, A, D
Page 22 .... D, A, D
Page 23 .... C, B, D
Page 24 .... B, A, C

2.OA.C.4

Page 25 .... A, C, A
Page 26 .... B, C, D
Page 27 .... A, B, A
Page 28 .... A, A, B
Page 29 .... D, A, B
Page 30 .... A, D, C
Page 31 .... B, B, A
Page 32 .... A, D, B

2.NBT.A.1

Page 33 .... B, B, A
Page 34 .... C, C, D
Page 35 .... C, A, B
Page 36 .... B, A, C
Page 37 .... D, D, B
Page 38 .... D, C, D
Page 39 .... A, A, B
Page 40 .... A, D, D

2.NBT.A.2

Page 41 .... C, A, C
Page 42 .... B, D, B
Page 43 .... B, B, B
Page 44 .... A, C, A
Page 45 .... C, B, D
Page 46 .... C, C, A
Page 47 .... C, C, D
Page 48 .... A, B, D

©Teachers' Treasures Publishing

ANSWER KEY

2.NBT.A.3

Page 49 .... A, C, B
Page 50 .... A, C, B
Page 51 .... C, A, D
Page 52 .... D, B, D
Page 53 .... B, C, D
Page 54 .... A, C, D
Page 55 .... A, A, D
Page 56 .... D, A, C

2.NBT.A.4

Page 57 .... A, B, C
Page 58 .... B, C, C
Page 59 .... B, B, A
Page 60 .... B, D, B
Page 61 .... B, C, B
Page 62 .... B, B, C
Page 63 .... C, B, A
Page 64 .... D, A, B

2.NBT.B.5

Page 65 .... B, A, C
Page 66 .... A, D, D
Page 67 .... C, D, B
Page 68 .... B, D, D
Page 69 .... B, A, A
Page 70 .... A, C, B
Page 71 .... C, A, B
Page 72 .... C, D, A

2.NBT.B.6

Page 73 .... B, A, B
Page 74 .... B, A, D
Page 75 .... C, A, A
Page 76 .... B, C, B
Page 77 .... A, C, D
Page 78 .... A, C, C
Page 79 .... D, A, C
Page 80 .... A, C, B

2.NBT.B.7

Page 81 .... D, A, C
Page 82 .... D, A, B
Page 83 .... D, A, A
Page 84 .... C, B, A
Page 85 .... C, B, A
Page 86 .... C, A, A
Page 87 .... C, D, A
Page 88 .... C, C, A

2.NBT.B.8

Page 89 .... A, C
Page 90 .... A, C, A
Page 91 .... A, C, B
Page 92 .... A, A, A
Page 93 .... D, B, B
Page 94 .... A, A, A
Page 95 .... B, B, A
Page 96 .... A, D, B

©Teachers' Treasures Publishing

ANSWER KEY

2.NBT.B.9

Page 97 .... D, C, A
Page 98 .... D, D, C
Page 99 .... A, C, D
Page 100 .... A, C, B
Page 101 .... C, A, D
Page 102 .... D, A, D
Page 103 .... C, B, B
Page 104 .... C, C, B

2.MD.A.1

Page 105 .... B, B, B
Page 106 .... A, D, C
Page 107 .... A, A, B
Page 108 .... D, D, A
Page 109 .... D, C, A
Page 110 .... D, A, B
Page 111 .... C, D, D
Page 112 .... C, B, A

2.MD.A.2

Page 113 .... B, D, A
Page 114 .... B, B, C
Page 115 .... A, D, A
Page 116 .... C, A, C
Page 117 .... B, A, C
Page 118 .... C, C, A
Page 119 .... B, C, A
Page 120 .... B, B, C

2.MD.A.3

Page 121 .... C, A, A
Page 122 .... B, A, D
Page 123 .... A, A, A
Page 124 .... A, B, D
Page 125 .... A, B, A
Page 126 .... C, C, D
Page 127 .... D, A, A
Page 128 .... C, B, D

2.MD.A.4

Page 129 .... B, C, A
Page 130 .... B, C, D
Page 131 .... B, A, B
Page 132 .... D, B, D
Page 133 .... C, A, B
Page 134 .... C, D, B
Page 135 .... D, D, C
Page 136 .... B, A, A

2.MD.B.5

Page 137 .... A, A, C
Page 138 .... C, A, A
Page 139 .... D, A, B
Page 140 .... A, D, B
Page 141 .... B, A, A
Page 142 .... B, D, B
Page 143 .... C, D, B
Page 144 .... C, A, B

©Teachers' Treasures Publishing

ANSWER KEY

2.MD.B.6

Page 145 ……… B, A, C
Page 146 ……… B, D, A
Page 147 ……… B, C, A
Page 148 ……… C, A, C
Page 149 ……… B, D, A
Page 150 ……… B, B, D
Page 151 ……… A, D, B
Page 152 ……… B, C, C

2.MD.C.7

Page 153 ……… B, D, C
Page 154 ……… C, C, D
Page 155 ……… A, C, A
Page 156 ……… C, D, A
Page 157 ……… D, C, B
Page 158 ……… A, A, C
Page 159 ……… B, D, B
Page 160 ……… B, C, D

2.MD.C.8

Page 161 ……… A, D, B
Page 162 ……… B, A, C
Page 163 ……… A, C, A
Page 164 ……… B, C, A
Page 165 ……… D, B, C
Page 166 ……… D, A, B
Page 167 ……… C, B, C
Page 168 ……… A, C, C

2.MD.D.9

Page 169 ……… A, B
Page 170 ……… D, D
Page 171 ……… C, D
Page 172 ……… A, D
Page 173 ……… A, D
Page 174 ……… A
Page 175 ……… C, B
Page 176 ……… B, B

2.MD.D.10

Page 177 ……… A, C
Page 178 ……… C, A
Page 179 ……… B, A, D
Page 180 ……… C, C
Page 181 ……… A, D
Page 182 ……… B, A
Page 183 ……… C, C
Page 184 ……… B, A

2.G.A.1

Page 185 ……… D, B, C
Page 186 ……… B, D, B
Page 187 ……… D, A, D
Page 188 ……… B, A, A
Page 189 ……… D, B, B
Page 190 ……… B, A, D
Page 191 ……… A, C, B
Page 192 ……… C, D, B

ANSWER KEY

2.G.A.2

Page 193 ……..... A, A, D
Page 194 ……..... C, B, C
Page 195 ……..... A, B, D
Page 196 ……..... C, D, B
Page 197 ……..... D, D, B
Page 198 ……..... C, D, B
Page 199 ……..... D, A, C
Page 200 ……..... A, D, B

2.G.A.3

Page 201 ……..... B, A, B
Page 202 ……..... A, B, B
Page 203 ……..... A, D, A
Page 204 ……..... D, A, A
Page 205 ……..... D, C, B
Page 206 ……..... C, B, B
Page 207 ……..... B, B, B
Page 208 ……..... B, C, B

©Teachers' Treasures Publishing

Made in the USA
Columbia, SC
25 May 2019